W9-AXL-053

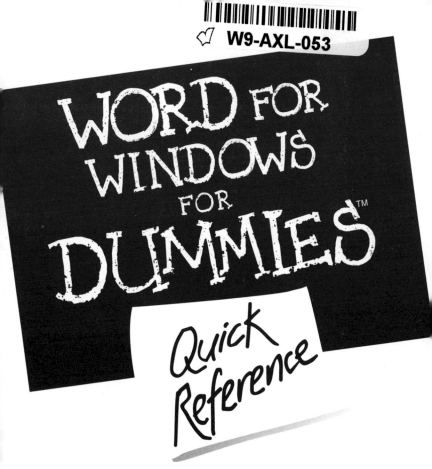

WORD FOR WINDOWS FOR DUMMIES™

Quick Reference

by George T. Lynch
Preface by Series Editor Dan Gookin

IDG BOOKS

IDG Books Worldwide, Inc.
An International Data Group Company

San Mateo, California ♦ Indianapolis, Indiana ♦ Boston, Massachusetts

Word for Windows For Dummies Quick Reference

Published by
IDG Books Worldwide, Inc.
An International Data Group Company
155 Bovet Road, Suite 310
San Mateo, CA 94402

Library of Congress Catalog Card No.: 93-78450

ISBN 1-56884-029-2

Printed in the United States of America

10 9 8 7 6 5 4 3 2 1

Distributed in the United States by IDG Books Worldwide, Inc.

Distributed in Canada by Macmillan of Canada, a Division of
Canada Publishing Corporation; by Woodslane Pty. Ltd. in Austra-
lia and New Zealand; and by Computer Bookshops in the U.K. and
Ireland.

For information on translations and availability in other countries,
contact Marc Jeffrey Mikulich, Foreign Rights Manager, at IDG
Books Worldwide; FAX NUMBER 415-358-1260.

For sales inquiries and special prices for bulk quantities, write to
the address above or call IDG Books Worldwide at 415-312-0650.

Acknowledgments

I would be remiss if I did not thank the many who helped me in the creation of this book. It is only fair to begin with my wife, Maureen, who willingly put our lives on hold and gave me great moral support while I worked on this manuscript. I'd also like to thank my friend and colleague, Don Gosselin, for picking up the slack when I couldn't and offering much-needed guidance. Thanks should also go to Belinda Rubino, Pam Holland, and Marilyn Arato of First Boston for their understanding patience with this project. Others who contributed in one form or another include Michael Dagley, Pico Nazzaro, and Steve Ryan, all experts to whom I often turn when I run into a blank wall. And I would also like to mention Scott Cunningham (for getting me to write in the first place), Craig Jennings, Juancho Clocon, Ray Tracy, Mark Read, and Harlan Lax for their support.

I'd also like to thank David Solomon and Janna Custer for giving me the opportunity to write this reference. And thanks would not be complete without acknowledging the encouragement and gentle prodding from the IDG editing team. Thanks to Mary Bednarek for her encouragement and interest in me as a writer. Finally, I think we must all thank Dan Gookin for creating this series. I know I do.

(The publisher would like to give special thanks to Patrick J. McGovern, without whom this book would not have been possible.)

Credits

Publisher
David Solomon

Acquisitions Editor
Janna Custer

Managing Editor
Mary Bednarek

Project Editors
Rebecca Whitney
H. Leigh Davis
Diane Graves Steele

Editors
Tracy Barr
Erik Dafforn
Kezia Endsley
Mary Corder

Technical Reviewer
Michael Partington

Production Manager
Beth J. Baker

Production Coordinator
Cindy L. Phipps

Production Staff
Tony Augsburger
Mary Breidenbach
Chris Collins
Drew R. Moore

Indexer
Sherry Massey

A Call to Readers:

We want to Hear From You!

Listen up, all you readers of IDG's *Word for Windows For Dummies Quick Reference.* It is time for you to take advantage of a new, direct pipeline for readers of IDG's international bestsellers — the famous . . . *For Dummies* books.

We would like your input for future printings and editions of this book. Tell us what you liked (and didn't like) about the *1-2-3 For Dummies Quick Reference.*

We'll add you to our *Dummies Database/Fan Club* and keep you up to date on the latest . . . *For Dummies* books, news, cartoons, calendars, and more!

Please send your name, address, and phone number, as well as your comments, questions, and suggestions, to:

. . . For Dummies Coordinator
IDG Books Worldwide
3250 North Post Road, Suite 140
Indianapolis, Indiana 46226

Thanks for your input!

About the Author

George Lynch, the author of two previous computer books, has been a computer training and development consultant in the New York City area for the past several years. His clients have included major investment and commercial banks, law firms, real estate companies, smaller businesses, and individuals. He is a certified professional in Windows, Word for Windows, and Excel. He has written numerous training manuals, articles, and user guides for clients, and he belongs to several computer organizations in the New York City area. (Face it — the guy is a certified computer nerd.)

About the Series Editor

Dan Gookin, the author of *DOS For Dummies, DOS For Dummies, 2nd Edition, WordPerfect For Dummies, WordPerfect 6 For Dummies,* and co-author of *PCs For Dummies* and the *Illustrated Computer Dictionary For Dummies,* is a writer and computer "guru" whose job is to remind everyone that computers are not to be taken too seriously. Presently, Mr. Gookin works for himself as a freelance writer. Gookin holds a degree in Communications from the University of California, San Diego, and is a regular contributor to *InfoWorld, PC/Computing, DOS Resource Guide,* and *PC Buying World* magazines.

About IDG Books Worldwide

Welcome to the world of IDG Books Worldwide.

IDG Books Worldwide, Inc., is a division of International Data Group, the world's largest publisher of computer-related information and the leading global provider of information services on information technology. IDG publishes over 194 computer publications in 62 countries. Forty million people read one or more IDG publications each month.

If you use personal computers, IDG Books is committed to publishing quality books that meet your needs. We rely on our extensive network of publications, including such leading periodicals as *Macworld, InfoWorld, PC World, Publish, Computerworld, Network World,* and *SunWorld,* to help us make informed and timely decisions in creating useful computer books that meet your needs.

Every IDG book strives to bring extra value and skill-building instruction to the reader. Our books are written by experts, with the backing of IDG periodicals, and with careful thought devoted to issues such as audience, interior design, use of icons, and illustrations. Our editorial staff is a careful mix of high-tech journalists and experienced book people. Our close contact with the makers of computer products helps ensure accuracy and thorough coverage. Our heavy use of personal computers at every step in production means we can deliver books in the most timely manner.

We are delivering books of high quality at competitive prices on topics customers want. At IDG, we believe in quality, and we have been delivering quality for over 25 years. You'll find no better book on a subject than an IDG book.

John Kilcullen
President and C.E.O.
IDG Books Worldwide, Inc.

IDG Books Worldwide, Inc. is a division of International Data Group. The officers are Patrick J. McGovern, Founder and Board Chairman; Walter Boyd, President. International Data Group's publications include: **ARGENTINA's** Computerworld Argentina, InfoWorld Argentina; **ASIA's** Computerworld Hong Kong, PC World Hong Kong, Computerworld Southeast Asia, PC World Singapore, Computerworld Malaysia, PC World Malaysia; **AUSTRALIA's** Computerworld Australia, Australian PC World, Australian Macworld, Network World, Reseller, IDG Sources; **AUSTRIA's** Computerwelt Oesterreich, PC Test; **BRAZIL's** Computerworld, Mundo IBM, Mundo Unix, PC World, Publish; **BULGARIA's** Computerworld Bulgaria, Ediworld, PC & Mac World Bulgaria; **CANADA's** Direct Access, Graduate Computerworld, InfoCanada, Network World Canada; **CHILE's** Computerworld, Informatica; **COLUMBIA's** Computerworld Columbia; **CZECH REPUBLIC's** Computerworld, Elektronika, PC World; **DENMARK's** CAD/CAM WORLD, Communications World, Computerworld Danmark, LOTUS World, Macintosh Produktkatalog, Macworld Danmark, PC World Danmark, PC World Produktguide, Windows World; **EQUADOR's** PC World; **EGYPT's** Computerworld (CW) Middle East, PC World Middle East; **FINLAND's** MikroPC, Tietoviikko, Tietoverkko; **FRANCE's** Distributique, GOLDEN MAC, InfoPC, Languages & Systems, Le Guide du Monde Informatique, Le Monde Informatique, Telecoms & Reseaux; **GERMANY's** Computerwoche, Computerwoche Focus, Computerwoche Extra, Computerwoche Karriere, Information Management, Macwelt, Netzwelt, PC Welt, PC Woche, Publish, Unit; **HUNGARY's** Alaplap, Computerworld SZT, PC World, ; **INDIA's** Computers & Communications; **ISRAEL's** Computerworld Israel, PC World Israel; **ITALY's** Computerworld Italia, Lotus Magazine, Macworld Italia, Networking Italia, PC World Italia; **JAPAN's** Computerworld Japan, Macworld Japan, SunWorld Japan, Windows World; **KENYA's** East African Computer News; **KOREA's** Computerworld Korea, Macworld Korea, PC World Korea; **MEXICO's** Compu Edicion, Compu Manufactura, Computacion/Punto de Venta, Computerworld Mexico, MacWorld, Mundo Unix, PC World, Windows; **THE NETHERLAND'S** Computer! Totaal, LAN Magazine, MacWorld; **NEW ZEALAND's** Computer Listings, Computerworld New Zealand, New Zealand PC World; **NIGERIA's** PC World Africa; **NORWAY's** Computerworld Norge, C/World, Lotusworld Norge, Macworld Norge, Networld, PC World Ekspress, PC World Norge, PC World's Product Guide, Publish World, Student Data, Unix World, Windowsworld, IDG Direct Response; **PANAMA's** PC World; **PERU's** Computerworld Peru, PC World; **PEOPLES REPUBLIC OF CHINA's** China Computerworld, PC World China, Electronics International, China Network World; **IDG HIGH TECH BEIJING's** New Product World; **IDG SHENZHEN's** Computer News Digest; **PHILLIPPINES'** Computerworld, PC World; **POLAND's** Computerworld Poland, PC World/ Komputer; **PORTUGAL's** Cerebro/PC World, Correio Informatico/Computerworld, MacIn; **ROMANIA's** PC World; **RUSSIA's** Computerworld-Moscow, Mir-PC, Sety; **SLOVENIA's** Monitor Magazine; **SOUTH AFRICA's** Computing S.A.; **SPAIN's** Amiga World, Computerworld Espana, Communications World, Macworld Espana, NeXTWORLD, PC World Espana, Publish, Sunworld; **SWEDEN's** Attack, ComputerSweden, Corporate Computing, Lokala Natverk/LAN, Lotus World, MAC&PC, Macworld, Mikrodatorn, PC World, Publishing & Design (CAP), Datalngenjoren, Maxi Data, Windows World; **SWITZERLAND's** Computerworld Schweiz, Macworld Schweiz, PC & Workstation; **TAIWAN's** Computerworld Taiwan, Global Computer Express, PC World Taiwan; **THAILAND's** Thai Computerworld; **TURKEY's** Computerworld Monitor, Macworld Turkiye, PC World Turkiye; **UNITED KINGDOM's** Lotus Magazine, Macworld, Sunworld; **UNITED STATES'** AmigaWorld, Cable in the Classroom, CD Review, CIO, Computerworld, Desktop Video World, DOS Resource Guide, Electronic News, Federal Computer Week, Federal Integrator, GamePro, IDG Books, InfoWorld, InfoWorld Direct, Laser Event, Macworld, Multimedia World, Network World, NeXTWORLD, PC Games, PC Letter, PC World, PC World Publish, Sumeria, SunWorld, SWATPro, Video Event; **VENEZUELA's** Computerworld Venezuela, MicroComputerworld Venezuela; **VIETNAM's** PC World Vietnam

Contents at a Glance

Preface

DOS For Dummies — and all the books in the *...For Dummies* series — are the ideal computer references. Have a problem? Great, look it up in *...For Dummies,* find out how to get it done right, and then close the book and return to your work. That's the way all computer books should work: quickly, painlessly, and with a dash of humor to keep the edge off.

So why is an Word for Windows quick reference needed? Yikes! Who wants to look at that junk? Who cares about tab leaders and toolbars? Chances are you might, someday.

The way we work with computers is that we often imitate what others do. Fred may hand you a document and say, "Add headers and footers to this 50-page document." Being suspicious—which is always good around Fred—you want to make sure you won't be doing anything disastrous. *Word for Windows For Dummies* can't help you weasel out commands that are way beyond the reach of the typical Dummy. So what you're left with is the Word for Windows manual or the fuzzy-headed on-line help.

Thank goodness for this book!

George Lynch has done the tedious job of transposing all the Word for Windows features from crypto-manual speak into a plain language reference we can use during those painful "must look it up in the manual" moments. He's peppered it with information, dos and don'ts, and the splash of humor you've come to expect from any book with *Dummies* on the title.

So tuck this reference in tight somewhere right by your PC. Keep it handy for when you must know the advanced options of some command or to confirm your worst fears about what it is Fred wants you to do to your own PC.

Dan Gookin

Word for Windows: Combining Ease of Use and Power

Welcome to the *Word for Windows For Dummies Quick Reference,* a guide that takes you through the most commonly used features of Word for Windows.

Word for Windows is a word-processing system, of course, which should mean that it processes words (whatever *that* means). But, as anyone who has tried to decipher any word-processing system can tell you, the real word processor is the person sitting at the keyboard. The system only provides the tools (programmers like to call tools *features*) for you to do the processing.

Word for Windows, as its name implies, is a word-processing system that uses *Windows* rather than just DOS. Remember that Windows is a graphical way of using your computer. *Graphical* means that you use a mouse and point at little cartoons — I mean, icons — rather than type a command. If you would decide that you don't want to use a graphical system, you would just use DOS. Word-processing systems are available for either type of environment. Word 5.0 and Word 5.5, for example, are versions of Word that do not use Windows.

The topic of this book, however, is Word for Windows. This book is divided into ten parts, and each part concentrates on specific areas of Word for Windows. Within each part are sections that discuss specific topics.

A Little about DOS and Windows

Because Word for Windows is a word-processing system de-signed to be used with Windows, it's necessary to begin by talking about Windows itself and what this means to you. And, to properly talk about Windows, we have to begin with DOS. (Have you ever noticed that, when it comes to computers, you can never talk about "this" without first talking about "that"? And you can't just start talking about "that" without mentioning "this other thing" first. That, unfortunately, is life with computers.)

Every computer needs an *operating system.* This term is used to describe the set of programs that makes the computer run. The operating system that has been around almost since the begin-ning of PCs is known as DOS (an acronym for *d*isk *o*perating system). (For more about DOS, see *DOS For Dummies* and the *DOS For Dummies Command Reference* in this series.) Although

other operating systems exist, IBM and IBM-compatible computers mostly use DOS as their operating system. This means that
most of the computing world has to know something about DOS.
Too bad, eh?

DOS is responsible for all areas of your computer's operation. It
keeps track of what's where. DOS is responsible for retrieving
your files when you want them, and for coordinating the elements
of your computer, such as translating those keystrokes into
something your computer understands and sending the correct
signals to the printer so that it prints what you want it to print.
DOS also handles other mysterious things, like memory, that we
do not delve into here. (Thank goodness!)

Programs you use to create documents (such as Word for
Windows) or spreadsheets (such as Lotus or Excel) are called
application software, or just *applications.* Application software
works with DOS to do such things as printing and file retrieval.
You don't have to worry, therefore, about how to figure out how
to use DOS to get these things done. The programmers who
created the application took care of these tasks (which is why
some programs do certain things better than other programs do
— they were written by better programmers). Instead, you have
to figure out how to do these things by using your application
(which can be tricky, but not as tricky as using DOS).

DOS has rightfully earned the reputation of being difficult to learn
and use, so most people would rather not deal with DOS if they
can avoid it. You cannot avoid DOS entirely, however, because it
plays a part in every operation of your computer. Enterprising
software companies, therefore, have created a type of software
known as *DOS shell* software. DOS shells are programs that
enable users (you) to work with DOS but not have to deal with its
difficulties. Instead, you learn how to use the shell and let it deal
with DOS. Some of these programs are quite good and have
become industry standards (XTree, the Norton Utilities, PC Tools,
and others). From these beginning arose Windows.

You can think of Windows as a kind of DOS shell because it is also
a way of using DOS. Windows is more than just the usual DOS
shell, however. You can do things when you use Windows that
you cannot do in DOS alone. In essence, Windows changes DOS
from a text-based system (where you type those mysterious
commands) to a graphics-based system (where you use a mouse
to point at pictures, also known as icons, and click). Also, when
you use Windows, you can run more than one application at a
time (depending on the configuration of your computer), unlike
when you use DOS alone. Windows also standardizes such things
as printing. Rather than your having to figure out how each
application prints, all applications that use Windows use exactly
the same print procedures. (Whew.)

Because application software that uses DOS alone had be rewritten to take advantage of Windows, we now have *Word for DOS* and *Word for Windows.* Most major software manufacturers now have Windows versions of their software packages, so you have to be careful if you decide to buy a program to use at home. If you use Windows, you want to be sure that the program you buy is a Windows program.

Windows Newcomers and Their Most Common Problems

When you first encounter Windows, you may wonder what all the fuss is about. You may become frustrated with its intricacies and feel overwhelmed by its complexity. Perseverance is what's needed here, however, because the more familiar you become with Windows, the more you appreciate its strengths and advantages. Remember that Windows is very powerful (which means that it can do lots of things) and that powerful software can take time to learn.

A fundamental principle of working in Windows is that *you must select whatever you want to work on before you work on it.* This principle is so important to working in Windows that it is mentioned many times throughout this book. It seems so simple, and yet....

In Word for Windows 2.0, you can move and copy text, copy formats, and accomplish other complex tasks by using the mouse alone (or sometimes in conjunction with a keystroke). You can learn more about how Word for Windows uses the mouse in the section "Using the Mouse" in Part I.

There is a reason that Windows is called Windows. You can (and mostly do) have multiple windows open at one time when you work in Windows. Almost everything you do is done in its own window. If you are working in Word for Windows, for example, you are in one window. If you decide to open Excel, you open another window. In traditional DOS-based software, only one window is open at a time — the one you are working in. If that window suddenly disappears, you have a problem.

In Windows, although you can have multiple windows open, you can work in only one window at a time. This window is cleverly called the *active window.* The quickest (but not the only) way to make any window the active window is simply to click once somewhere in that window (assuming that you can see a part of it).

There is little you can do to hurt yourself (unless you make a series of missteps). Having that enormous file you haven't saved for the last four hours disappear from the screen may cause your heart to skip a beat, but, unless you see some kind of message from the system, the file is probably still open and waiting for you to come back to it. (If you inadvertently turn off your computer, Word for Windows has an *autoclave* feature to get around this disaster (see the section "Saving Files" in Part III).

Another source of frustration to new Windows users is that there are at least two ways to accomplish most things, and as many as four or five ways to accomplish some tasks. In Word for Windows, for example, there are at least four different ways to paste text or graphics into a document. There are also three different ways to set the left and right margins.

No particular way is better or worse than any other particular way to do something. Most actions in Word for Windows can be accomplished by using either the mouse or the keyboard.

How Do I Use This Book?

Like any technical book, the best place to begin when you want to find a specific topic is at the index. You can also skim the table of contents to refresh your memory about the various topics and to see how the book is organized. Within the book are various icons (listed at the end of the Introduction) so that you can see at a glance what to avoid and what might be safe and helpful. Most users of word-processing systems try something and, if it doesn't work, they panic. Let me suggest that you first consult this Quick Reference. It not only reduces the frequency of errors but also reduces the amount and intensity of your panic.

This book progresses from general topics (a description of the screen and using the keyboard, for example) to specific topics (file management, formatting, tables, and so on). The earlier chapters are for those who are brand new to Word for Windows; if you have some familiarity with this program, you can proceed to the later chapters.

Because Word for Windows is a graphical word-processing system and because the mouse is an increasingly important element, all the instructions in this book assume that you use the mouse. However, I have included keystrokes for tasks in which a keystroke may be more efficient and easier to use.

For diehard keystroke aficionados, Part X lists all the important keystrokes in Word for Windows.

The Cast of Icons

The following icons appear throughout this book to help point out important information. They instantly tell you a few key things about each command.

Probably worth your while to learn about this command.

Normally used only by advanced Word for Windows users or for special purposes; can be useful at times.

Generally not used by beginners, but you may have to use this command anyway.

Indicates that a command is safe for your data (worst case is another error message).

Generally safe in most circumstances, unless you don't follow instructions (look out!).

Potentially dangerous to data but necessary in the scheme of things; *be careful* with this command.

A problem area that can mess up your work if you don't stay on your toes; something in this command can get you in trouble.

Alerts you to a way of using a command that may not be immediately obvious to average users.

A little information that can be stored away deep inside your brain.

Flags cross references to other areas of this book that might be of interest to you.

Tells you where to look in *Word for Windows For Dummies* for more information; if you don't have that book, don't bother reading this stuff.

Problem area that can mess up your work if you don't stay on your toes.

Part 1
The Word for Windows Basics

This part of the book describes the Word for Windows screen, the keyboard, the mouse, and the different views available to you in Word for Windows. If you feel comfortable with this stuff already, you might want to skip to other parts of the book. On the other hand, you might learn some things that you didn't know. And, you might find answers to those annoying things that seem to keep happening to you for no apparent reason.

One major principle to keep in mind when you work with Word for Windows is that you must select whatever you want to work on before you work on it. If you want to bold that sentence, for example, you have to select it first. If you don't, you will be surprised (sometimes unpleasantly) to see that the sentence remains unchanged while some other selection does become bolded. This principle always applies.

This principle leads us to an equally important principle: If you try to do something and it doesn't happen, immediately Undo whatever it was you did. Just because what you wanted to do didn't occur doesn't mean that *something* didn't happen. You can save yourself lots of grief if you can remember this statement. You can always undo your last action by clicking Edit Undo or pressing Ctrl+Z. Undo works only on your last action, though, so if you decide several steps later that you should have undone that first step, it's too late. You have to undo that first step manually. Fortunately, Undo works as a toggle: If you undo an action and then decide that it should not have been undone, you can undo the undo. (Really, it works.)

The Parts of the Screen

The following two illustrations show the Word for Windows screen in its full glory. The only difference between the two is that in the first figure the document window is maximized and in the second figure the document screen is not maximized. You might prefer to work with the document window maximized to gain the maximum amount of space on your monitor.

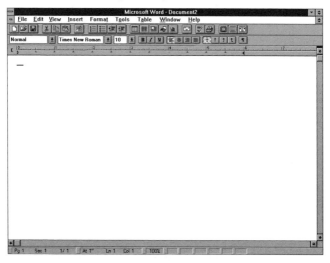

The top portion of the two figures contains most of the tools you work with in Word for Windows. It contains these five elements:

- Title bar
- Menu bar
- Toolbar
- Ribbon
- Ruler

The following figure shows the parts of the Word for Windows screen: the title bar, menu bar, toolbar, ribbon, control and sizing buttons, scroll buttons, and ruler.

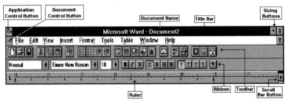

 For more information on the Word for Windows screen, see Chapter 1 in *Word for Windows for Dummies.*

The title bar

From the title bar, you can easily see both the application being used and the file that is open. To the left of the title bar is the control menu button. If you·click once on this button, a pull-down menu appears. One of the options on this menu is Close, a method you can use to close the entire application (not just the file that is open).

 You can close almost any Windows application, including Windows itself, by simply double-clicking on the control menu button.

To the right of the title bar is a cluster of buttons. The down-pointing button is the Minimize button (the little devil that gets so many newcomers in trouble). When you click once on this button, Word for Windows becomes an icon and disappears from your screen. Every window in Windows has a Minimize button. Use it when you want to do something else but not close your application.

 If Word for Windows suddenly disappears with no warning messages, you probably have clicked the Minimize button. You can see whether Word for Windows is still open by pressing Ctrl+Esc. This step produces the Task List. If Word for Windows is still open, it is on this list. You can get your Word for Windows screen back by first selecting Word for Windows and then clicking the Switch To button.

The menu bar

Word for Windows keeps its menus, cleverly enough, on the menu bar. Each menu item has one underlined letter. You can use this letter to gain access to that menu. Just press Alt and the letter for the particular menu. Or just click on the menu selection with the mouse.

The toolbar

The toolbar, which sits just below the menu bar, consists entirely of buttons (or tools, as Microsoft prefers to have you think of them). In this nifty feature, each of the buttons performs some sort of function when you click once on it. The first button, for example, is the File New button. If you click once on this button, a new document opens. This document is based on the Normal template.

The ribbon

The ribbon is just under the toolbar and above the ruler. The ribbon contains a shortcut feature in much the same manner as the toolbar, except that it has drop-down (or *cascading*) lists for styles, fonts, and font sizes.

The ruler

The ruler is another tool you can use instead of wading through the menus to accomplish a task. You can use the ruler to set and change tabs, indents, and the left and right margins in your document.

The scroll bars

In addition to the tools mentioned, the Word for Windows screen also contains scroll bars (see the following figure). The vertical scroll bar enables you to scroll up and down through your document, and the horizontal scroll bar enables you to scroll left and right.

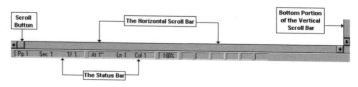

The scroll bar button can tell you at a glance where you are in your document. If you have a document on-screen and the vertical scroll bar button is in the middle of the scroll bar, you are in the middle of your document. To move quickly to the beginning, the end, or somewhere in the middle of a document, you can click and drag on the button to the appropriate spot and release the mouse button.

The status bar

The status bar, at the bottom of the Word for Windows screen, displays the page number, section number, and total page count. It also shows what percentage of the normal size of your document you are using to view the document.

You can also see small rectangles to the right of the percentage. Each of these areas displays certain information about what is happening. If you press the Ins key on your keyboard, for example, you change from insert mode to overtype mode (in which you replace existing characters as you type). Also, the letters OVR appear in one of the boxes in the status bar to inform you that you are in overtype mode.

To turn off the scroll bars and the status bar, choose Options from the Tools menu to open the Tools Options dialog box. To turn off the scroll bars or the status bar, just clear the appropriate check box by clicking once in it.

At the bottom of this dialog box, you can opt to work with a blank screen. If you don't like the blank look, press Esc and the screen returns to normal. You can still use the menus when you decide to work with a full screen if you know the keyboard assignments (when you press Alt+F, for example, the File pull-down menu appears).

The Keyboard

Word for Windows is a graphical word-processing system that uses the mouse extensively. You cannot forget about the keyboard, however. For one thing, you still have to type your document, so typing hasn't become obsolete. Yet. Let's begin with a few words (OK, more than a few) about using a computer keyboard.

 For more information on the keyboard, see Chapter 3 of *Word for Windows For Dummies*.

The keyboard on a computer

Two basic types of keyboards are in use today (although more and different types seem on the horizon): the original IBM PC keyboard, which has 10 gray F keys arranged vertically on the left side of the keyboard, and the enhanced keyboard, which has 12 F keys usually arranged horizontally across the top of the keyboard. Other than the number of keys on the keyboard and the two extra F keys, there really isn't any functional difference between the two.

Most computer keyboards still use the familiar QWERTY arrangement we all have come to know and love, so you can still impress friends and neighbors with your manual dexterity.

There are many other keys out there, however. What do they do? They do a lot. Let's look at some of them.

The F keys

The F keys are function keys (which is why they're called the F keys). The F keys have different functions depending on the software you are using. So the F3 key in Word for Windows, for example, is different from the F3 key in WordPerfect.

Most of the computer industry has settled on the F1 key as a help key. This agreement is fortunate — if you get stuck in some software and don't know what else to do, you can always press F1. Ninety-nine times out of a hundred, some form of help appears on-screen.

The combination keys (Alt, Ctrl, Shift)

Three combination keys are on the keyboard: Alt, Ctrl, and Shift. I call them combination keys because they are always used in combination with other keys — never alone. In essence, these keys change the function of other keys. So Alt+F1 is different from Shift+F1.

The proper way to use combination keys is to first press the combination key or keys (remember, some functions require two combination keys in conjunction with another key, such as Alt+Ctrl+Del to reboot). You can hold these keys down as long as you want and nothing happens until you press some other key. After you press the correct combination key (or keys), press the other key. At this point, you can release the combination keys.

Pressing the Ctrl or Shift keys by themselves produces no result at all. If you press the Alt key, however, you make the menu bar active. You can test this by pressing Alt and then pressing either the down-arrow or the right-arrow key and watching the menu bar.

If the menu bar is already active or a pull-down menu is displayed, you can close them by pressing Alt once. (You cannot close a dialog box, however, just by pressing Alt.)

The Esc key

When you don't know what else to do, you can always press the Esc key. Sometimes it even works. You can quickly close a dialog box you opened by mistake, for example, by pressing Esc. You can also close pull-down menus by pressing Esc; if you press it only once, however, the menu bar still is active. You must press it a second time to deactivate the menu bar entirely.

If you find yourself staring at the screen and you don't know what to do next, try pressing Esc. Maybe the problem in front of you will just disappear. (Hey, you can hope, can't you?) If that doesn't work, try pressing F1. If that doesn't work, call your computer geek friend (everyone should have one).

The numeric keypad and the Num Lock key

You may have noticed, on the right side of your keyboard, a set of gray keys and a set of white keys with numbers on them. If you look closely at the numbered keys, you see that they have not only a number but also another label (the 7 key, for example, also says "Home," and the 9 key also says "PgUp."

The trick is to make up your mind how you want to use the white keys. If you want to use them to type in numbers, just be sure that the Num Lock light is on. When the Num Lock light is on, those keys act as number keys. When the Num Lock light is not on, those keys act as whatever the other label indicates.

If you prefer to use those keys as number keys, you can use the gray keys just to the left instead to perform the other functions. Talk about overkill.

The numbered keys on the right side of the keyboard (as opposed to those above the top row of letters) are referred to as the *numeric keypad.* You may occasionally run software that instructs you to be sure that the Num Lock light is on and to use the numeric keypad for some function or another. If that is the case, you must use the numeric keypad, because using the numbers above the letters does not work. Fortunately, these types of instructions are few and far between, and whenever you run across them, they are usually well defined.

Keystrokes to cultivate

Even though the mouse is an important tool in Word for Windows, you may find some pretty nifty keystrokes that you really like (see the following table).

Keystroke	Meaning	Comments
F1	Help	Press F1 at any time to make a Help screen appear.
Shift+F1	Help on	Causes a question mark to attach itself to pointer the pointer on-screen. Point to any item or open a dialog box to get help on that item or dialog box.
F2 (first highlight the text to be moved)	Move	Move to where? appears in the status bar. You can move the insertion point (cursor) to the proper place in the document and press Enter to move the selection to the new place.
F2 (first move the insertion point to where you want to move the selection)	Move	Move from where? appears in the status bar. You can then find the text to be moved and select it. A dotted underline appears under all the text you select to be moved. After you have made your selection, press Enter.
Shift+F2	Copy	Works just like the Move keys described earlier, except that this functions copies the text instead of moving it.
Shift+F3	Toggle case	One of Word for Windows' best keystrokes!
		Select the text and then press Shift+F3.
		Pressing it once makes the selection all uppercase; pressing it again makes the selection all lowercase; pressing it a third time capitalizes the first letter of each word in the selection.
F4	Repeat key	F4 repeats your last action, whether you typed a sentence or formatted some text. It's a nice keystroke when you want to scroll through your document and boldface or italicize certain portions of the text. You must format normally the first time, but you can press F4 for each instance thereafter.

(continues)

Keystroke	Meaning	Comments
F5	GoTo	Another powerful key. If you press F5 once, the status bar displays GoTo:; if you press it twice, the GoTo dialog box is displayed. See Part IV for a full explanation of this keystroke.
F7	Spell checker	The spell checker checks the entire document unless you highlight text; in that case, it checks only the high-lighted selection.
Shift+F7	Thesaurus	Try it.
F8	Extend	Press F8 once to turn on the extend feature (you can see it in the status bar). You then can use your arrow keys to extend the selection. Press F8 twice to select the current word (where the insertion point is); press F8 three times to select the current sentence; press F8 four times to select the current paragraph; press F8 five times to select the entire document. See Part IV for an explanation of how to use the F8 key with the F5 key.
Shift+F12	Save	Quickly saves your document. If you haven't saved it before and it doesn't have a name, this keystroke opens the File Save dialog box. Otherwise, it updates the changes.
Ctrl+Z	Undo	An important keystroke.
Ctrl+5 (Numeric keypad)	Select All	Selects the entire document. Remember that you *must* use the numeric keypad on the right side of the keyboard in order for this keystroke to select the entire document. It doesn't make any difference whether the Num Lock light is on. (If you press the wrong 5 key, you will be surprised to see that you have changed the line spacing in whatever paragraph the insertion point happened to be in at the moment.)

(continues)

Keystroke	Meaning	Comments
Ctrl+Home	Beginning of document	This keystroke moves the insertion to the beginning of the document, no matter how large or small the document.
Ctrl+End	End of document	Moves the insertion point to the end of the document.
Ctrl+Enter	Page break	Inserts a hard page break at the insertion point.

Keystrokes to avoid

Fortunately, there aren't many keystrokes to avoid in Word for Windows. The following table lists keystrokes that may cause you a moment of panic because of the drastic change that can occur on your screen. The good news is that there isn't much you can do with keystrokes to hurt yourself. Just be sure that you carefully read any messages that suddenly appear on-screen, especially if they ask you about saving your work. If you're not sure, press Esc.

Keystroke	Meaning	Comments
Alt+F4	Quit Word for Windows	Nothing wrong with this keystroke, unless you don't mean to quit Word for Windows. If you haven't saved your work, you get a message asking whether you want to save your work. If you answer No, you lose all your unsaved work. Be careful if you suddenly get this type of message.
Ctrl+F4	Close active document	Again, there's nothing wrong with this keystroke if you want to close the document. The same warning applies here as above.
Alt+F5	Restore Word for Windows window	If you are running Word for Windows in a maximized window, this keystroke suddenly reduces the size of the window. This may not be a problem, but it also might cause you to panic. You can correct this situation, if it occurs, by pressing Alt+F10.

The Mouse

This section discusses the mouse — a device that seems to polarize users. Some love it and some hate it. However you feel about the mouse, I urge you to at least try some of the mouse procedures listed here.

Most people who don't like using a mouse change their minds in most cases when they gain some experience with it. Do yourself a favor: Play with the mouse from time to time and you might find that you're developing a grudging respect for this precision pointing device.

Everyone's favorite use of the mouse is Solitaire. In fact, Microsoft promotes Solitaire as a mouse learning aid. If you can use the mouse successfully with Solitaire, you should have no trouble using the mouse with Word for Windows.

Using the mouse to select text

One fundamental principle of working in any Windows software is that you first must select the text you want to modify before you perform your actions. This statement is also true in Word for Windows. To delete a sentence, you first must select the sentence. To underline a character in a word, you first must select that character. To italicize a paragraph, you first must select that paragraph, and so on.

The terms _select_ and _highlight_ are used interchangeably in this book and in general. When you highlight text, you select it. When you select text, you highlight it.

Want more information on selecting text? See Chapter 6 in _Word for Windows For Dummies._

The mouse buttons

Almost every mouse action in Word for Windows requires the left button. You might have to use combination keys in conjunction with the mouse, but rarely, if ever, do you have to use the right button.

The right button performs two functions — one when you work in tables (see Part V for more information about selecting in tables with the mouse) and the other with normal text. When you work with normal text, the right button performs a "column select" function. If you want to select, for example, a column in a table you created by using tabs rather than the table function, you can position the mouse pointer at the top of that column, press the right button, and drag to select the column. You might want to try this technique with a small table to get a feel for it.

Selecting with the mouse

Perhaps the biggest advantage of using the mouse is that it moves the insertion point (cursor) and selects text quickly and easily, after you learn a few tricks. It may help to keep a few things in mind about selecting text, whether it's with the mouse or the keyboard.

First, you can think of selecting text as expanding the insertion point to include the text. You always begin selecting text by moving the insertion point to the spot where the selection begins. Then, whether you use the mouse or the keyboard, the insertion point expands to highlight the selection.

Also, to remove a selection (or de-highlight, if you will), all you have to do is either click somewhere in the document or press one of the arrow keys. This method removes the highlight from the selected text and returns the flashing vertical insertion point.

You can use the techniques described in the following table to select portions of text quickly. You can combine some selection techniques with dragging also. The table instructs you to select a sentence, for example, by pointing at the sentence, pressing Ctrl, and then clicking. If you click and drag instead, you extend the selection a sentence at a time rather than a character at a time. Go ahead and experiment.

Mouse Action	*Comments*
Moving the insertion point with the mouse	Remember that the insertion point is the narrow blinking thing (I-beam) that used to be called a cursor. It shows you where you are in your document. You can always move the insertion point by using the arrow and other keys, but the mouse moves the insertion point quickly, accurately, and efficiently (if you use the mouse correctly).
	To move the insertion point with the mouse, simply point at the spot in the document where you want the insertion point to be located and click once. That's all there is to it.
Selecting text in general	Move the mouse pointer to the beginning of the text to be selected, press the left mouse button, and drag.
	Or place the insertion point at the beginning of the text to be selected, point to the end of the text to be selected *without clicking* (if you click, you move the insertion point), press Shift, and click the left mouse button once.

(continues)

Mouse Action	Comments
Selecting a word	Point at the word to be selected and then double-click the left mouse button. This method selects not only the word but also the space after the word (unless it is the last word in a sentence).
Selecting a sentence	Point anywhere in the sentence. Press Ctrl and click the left mouse button. (**Hint:** Because this technique looks for a period, if the sentence contains a period somewhere (Mr. Smith, for example), the selection stops at that period.)
Selecting a line of text	Move the pointer to the left of the left margin (so that the pointer becomes an arrow pointing toward the upper right) and then click the left mouse button once.
Selecting a paragraph	Move the mouse pointer to left of the paragraph (so that the pointer becomes an arrow pointing toward the upper right) and double-click the left mouse button.
Selecting the entire document	Move the mouse pointer to the left of any paragraph (so that the pointer becomes an arrow pointing toward the upper right) and then press Ctrl and click the left mouse button once.

Other useful mouse actions

In addition to using the mouse to select, you can use it in conjunction with combination keys to perform other actions, such as copying and moving text, copying formats, and opening dialog boxes. The following table lists some of the more useful mouse functions.

Mouse Action	Comments
Move text	First select the text. Then move the mouse pointer into the selected text until the pointer becomes an arrow pointing toward the upper left. Click and drag to the new position (notice the outline of the pointer during the drag operation). This process is known as *drag and drop*. Release the mouse button at the new position to finish the move.

(continues)

	Or select the text and then point to the new position without clicking. Press Ctrl and press the *right* mouse button.
Copy text	First select the text. Then move the mouse pointer into the selected text until the pointer becomes an arrow pointing toward the upper left. Press Ctrl and then click and drag to the new position (notice the outline of the pointer during the drag operation). Release the mouse button at the new position to finish the copy.
	Or select the text and then point to the new position without clicking. Press Ctrl+Shift and then click the *right* clicker once.
Copy formatting	Select the text you want to format. Point directly at the text that is already formatted the way you want without clicking. Press Ctrl+Shift and then press the *left* button.
Format character	Place the mouse pointer arrow on the ribbon *but not on an icon* (place the arrow on a blank spot on the ribbon) and double-click the left mouse button. This step opens the Format Character dialog box.
Format paragraph	Place the mouse pointer arrow on the upper half of the ruler (above the horizontal line) and double-click the left mouse button. This step opens the Format Paragraph dialog box.
Format section layout	Point at any section break (the thin double lines that run horizontally across the document) and double-click the left mouse button. This method opens the Format Section Layout dialog box. If you have only one section in your document, of course, you cannot perform this function (there are no section breaks).
Edit GoTo	Point at the status bar at the bottom of the screen and double-click the left mouse button. This technique opens the GoTo dialog box.

Various Views

Word for Windows provides a number of different ways for you to look at your document on-screen. Microsoft probably did this just to confuse you. No, you probably will use most of these views at some time or another. If not, who cares? You might, if you accidentally stumble into one of these views and wonder what the heck happened.

Normal view

Thank goodness for normal view. This default view is the one most of us prefer to use. When you are in normal view, you can see most things about your document, but you cannot see more than one page at a time, nor can you see headers, footers, or footnotes. You also cannot see newspaper-style columns side by side in normal view.

You can check which view you are in by clicking on the View menu. You can also choose other views from the View menu.

Page layout view

Page layout view shows the entire page as it will print. You can see headers, footers, footnotes, and all the rest in this view. So why not use it all the time? You can, if you want. The problem is that it is the most demanding view in terms of system resources (it slows your system down considerably). That's perhaps the biggest reason that most users prefer to work in normal view.

Some users get a little confused the first time they use page layout view because they see a horizontal line running across the screen at the top of the document. Not to worry: This is the top of the page. If you scroll down, the line disappears. If you keep scrolling, though, the bottom of the page soon comes into view, so you are faced with another line.

When you turn on page layout view, notice that a couple of new buttons appear at the bottom of the vertical scroll bar. One button has two arrowheads pointing up, and the other has two arrowheads pointing down. You can use these arrowheads to scroll a page at a time rather than line by line.

Draft mode

Draft mode is the least "viewer friendly" of the different display modes. So, you ask, why is it there? The use of draft mode when you work on a large complex document that contains graphics and other unusual elements can speed up your computer's processing considerably. The reason is that draft mode does not display graphics; instead, it just shows an outline of where the graphic will appear in the document. Also, draft mode does not display formatting. All formatting shows up as underlined.

If you suddenly realize, when you format text, that all the formatting is showing as underlined only, don't panic. This situation just means that you are in draft mode. You can turn draft mode on and off by selecting it from the Yiew menu. You can always tell that draft mode is on if a checkmark appears next to it.

Outline view

If you work on long, complicated documents, outline view is a specialized view you can use quickly to help you create outlines and tables of contents. Most people never use outline view except when they accidentally stumble into it. When you turn on outline view, the ruler is replaced by the outlining toolbar. If you have to work with these type of documents, using the outline features of Word for Windows is very helpful.

Using this feature by accident can cause panic because of the drastically different way it displays your document. Do yourself a favor and take a look at outline view when you are working on a document — not so much to use it as to become familiar with the way it looks so that you don't panic if you turn it on by mistake.

If you suddenly find yourself in outline view, simply choose either Normal or Page Layout from the Yiew menu. Because this is such a specialized feature, it is not covered in detail in this book.

Print preview

Print preview is not a view of the document in the same sense as the preceding views, but it is included in this part of the book because it is another way to look at your document. Print preview has a couple of unique characteristics:

- It is the only view in which you can see two pages at a time.

- You cannot perform any editing actions in print preview with the exception of changing the margins and adjusting certain types of page breaks.

You can open print preview by choosing Print Preyiew from the File menu.

Notice that a preview toolbar also appears at the top of a print preview screen. You can use the Print button to print the document while you are in print preview. The Margins button toggles the existing margins off and on. The next button toggles the print preview between one and two pages, and the Cancel button returns you to the previous view of your document (normal, page layout, or outline view).

You can move through your document in print preview by pressing PgDn and PgUp on the keyboard or by clicking on the vertical scroll bar. While you are in print preview, you can also use Ctrl+Home to move to the first page of your document, and Ctrl+End to move to the last page of the document.

Zooming

The zooming feature in Word for Windows enables you to magnify the document or reduce it in viewing size. Understand that this feature has no effect whatsoever on the *document*. If you think of looking at something through a magnifying glass, you know that the something doesn't change — your *view* of it changes. The same is true of using the zooming feature in Word for Windows.

You can zoom in or out on your document by choosing Zoom from the View menu. This step opens the Zoom dialog box, in which you can choose the size you want to use to view the document.

 The toolbar also has buttons you can use to change the magnification of your document, but they don't offer as much flexibility as does the dialog box. See Part II for an explanation of the buttons on the toolbar.

Using Multiple Windows

As a word-processing system designed for use with Windows, Word for Windows enables you to have multiple documents open at the same time. It also enables you to open multiple windows on the same document. Don't get confused here. Having multiple windows open for the same document is not the same as opening multiple documents. If you open a second document, you have two files open. If you open a second window on the same document, you still have only one file open.

Multiple windows on the same document

Why would you want to open multiple windows for the same document? You might want to move text from one area in your document to a different area and want to see both areas at the same time. You might want to use page layout in one window and normal mode in the other. Even if you don't want to have more than one window on a document open, it helps to know that you can. That way, if you inadvertently open more than one window on the same document, you have some idea of what has happened.

The confusing thing about all this is the question of making changes when you have more than one window with the same document. If you make a change in window one, does that change what happens in the other windows? The answer is yes, if those windows contain the same document. Remember that because you have only one file open, when you make a change to that file, the change happens in all windows that are open on that file.

You can have as many as nine windows open at one time in Word for Windows. This number includes multiple windows on the same document as well as other documents you may have open. If you open a second (or subsequent) window on the same document, the filename in the title bar shows a colon followed by a number (see the following figure). This number is the number of that window for the document. The figure also shows the same file in view in both windows at the same time.

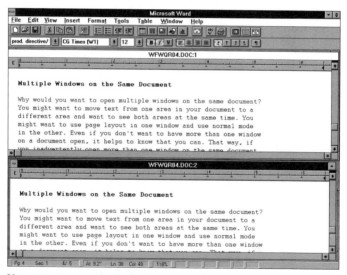

You can open multiple windows on the same documents in either of two ways: You can choose the same file again from the File menu or you can choose New Window from the Window menu. The Window menu also lists all the currently open windows, so you can select whichever window you want by clicking on that window in the Window menu.

Multiple windows on different documents

It is probably far more useful to have more than one document open at a time rather than multiple windows on the same document. You can open as many as nine different documents (as long as you don't have multiple windows open on any of them). You can use the Window menu to select the particular file you want at any given moment, or you can use the Arrange All option to show all open windows at the same time. The following figure shows four different files that are open and two windows for one of those files.

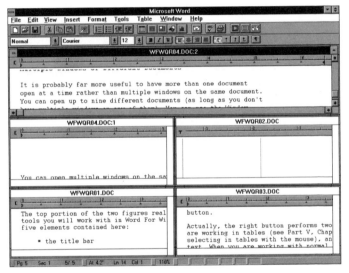

If you try to open more than nine windows, you get an error message. There really isn't much reason to have that many windows open at one time. Try to develop the good housekeeping habit of closing files and windows when you finish with them rather than leave them open. This practice may take a little time to get used to if your old word processor automatically closed open files when you opened a new one.

Panes

Panes? What the heck are panes? Here you are using Windows, so now you should learn a little about panes. Window panes — get it? Yuck.

Panes are similar to mini-windows. Some features in Word for Windows use panes rather than have you open a new window or change from normal to page layout view.

Remember earlier when I said that some things (such as headers and footers) are not visible in normal view? So what happens if you want to enter a header or footer? You can switch to page layout view or just go ahead and insert the header or footer without switching to page layout view. If you remain in normal view, a header or footer pane opens (see Part IV). Here, you can enter the header or footer. Panes also appear for footnotes and some other items in normal view.

You can read more about headers, footers, and footnotes in Part IV.

Part II
Using Those Menus

In discussing the basics of Word for Windows in Part I, we took a cursory look at some of these items. In this part of the book we will examine these features in more detail. Chapters 5 through 8 cover each of these features separately.

The menus in Word for Windows give you access to all of the features available. You can use the toolbar, the ribbon, and the ruler as shortcut tools to do a task, but you can also use the menus. The shortcuts provided by the other tools are incremental in most cases. That is, it doesn't take much more effort to use a menu to open a dialog box in order to bold selected text than to click the "B" button on the ribbon. For this reason, it might be advantageous for you to start by learning what the menu bar has to offer. Once you get the idea of how WinWord works, you can try the various shortcut methods. But, that is up to you. No matter which method you use, the result should be the same.

Sometimes the choice you want on a menu may not be available (it is grayed out). This happens because of the elements of your document when you opened the menu. If you select the Edit menu, for example, and Cut and Copy are not available, it is because you didn't select any text before opening the menu.

 Each menu and each option have one underlined letter. You can open the drop-down menu by pressing Alt and the underlined key. You can choose menu options just by typing the underlined letter (no Alt key is required). You may find this technique is quicker in many cases.

Some pull-down menu options have keystrokes listed to the right. You can use this keystroke rather than use the menu. The keystroke does not work if you first open the drop-down menu; you must use the keystroke or use the menu — not both.

Some menu options have three dots after them, known as an ellipsis. Options that show the three dots generate a dialog box if you choose them, so you have more choices to make.

 The tables in this part show the default menus. Sometimes a menu choice may change, depending on the circumstances of your document before you selected the menu. The choices change most often on the Table menu, which offers options depending on the type of table and what you selected before you selected the Table menu. This feature is one you may not even notice.

The File Menu

The File menu, naturally enough, gives you access to file management in Word for Windows. You can use this menu to create new files, to open existing files, and more.

The following list briefly explains each of the File menu options:

- **New...:** Shows the File New dialog box, which enables you to choose a template for your new file. (See Part III for more information about templates.)
- **Open...:** Shows a dialog box that lets you move around to different drives and directories to look for your file to open.
- **Close:** Closes the active file (the file you are working on). If you haven't saved your changes, Word for Windows prompts you.
- **Save:** Enables you to save your work. The first time you save a file, a dialog box opens so that you can name the file and store it in the proper directory.
- **Save As...:** Enables you to save the current file with a new name. This option is useful when you want to keep the old document as well as make changes to it.

- **Save All:** Saves changes to all open files, templates, glossaries, and macros, if any, in one step.

- **Find File...:** Opens a complicated dialog box that lets you search for files in a number of different ways if you have forgotten the name of the file. Using this dialog box takes some practice.

- **Summary Info...:** Displays a dialog box in which you can enter information about the current file. You can search on this information later by using File Find File.

- **Template...:** Lets you see which template the current document is using. Also enables you to change the template.

- **Print Preview:** Shows the print preview window, in which you can view your document before sending it to print.

- **Print...:** Shows a dialog box in which you can make choices about printing the current file.

- **Print Merge...:** Use this option when you want to create a merge. See Part VI for more information about merges.

- **Print Setup...:** Displays a dialog box in which you can select different printers if they have previously been installed. (You install printers through Windows, not through Word for Windows. If you want more information about this topic, consult your Windows documentation.)

- **Exit:** Closes Word for Windows. You are prompted about each file you have open that you haven't saved.

- **Numbers at the bottom of the menu:** A Word for Windows feature lists the last four files you worked on. If the file you want is one of the last four you worked on, rather than have to use File Open, you can just select it here with a mouse click.

The Edit Menu

The Edit menu contains some of the more interesting features in Word for Windows. Some, such as Find, Replace, and Glossary, can be real time-savers if you learn how to use them. I have been surprised at the small number of users who understand these quality-of-life procedures, especially because they are not difficult to learn (at least for us nerds). The following list explains each of the Edit menu options.

- **Undo:** Undoes your last action. Notice that it often states what it is undoing (Undo Typing or Undo Undo). If you want to undo something you did several (or just two) steps ago, you are out of luck, so be careful.

- **Repeat:** Repeats the last action. This option can be a blessing if you are repeating lots of formats, for example. The keystroke (F4) is much easier to use. Try it — you'll like it. (Sometimes, though, for unexplained reasons, the F4 key doesn't repeat what you want it to, so you have to do it by hand. Big deal — it's still a great keystroke.)

• **Cut:** Removes selected text you previously highlighted and places it in the Clipboard. (You remember the Clipboard, don't you? It is the Windows — not Word for Windows — device that acts as a storage buffer. You cut or copy something to the Clipboard and paste somewhere in a document whatever is in the Clipboard. Cutting or copying something new to the Clipboard replaces whatever was there before.)

• **Copy:** Acts the same as Cut, except that it doesn't remove the selected text from the original area.

• **Paste:** You use this option to get the stuff from the Clipboard and put it in your document. Just place the insertion point where you want to insert the stuff that's in the Clipboard. (**Note:** Whatever is in the Clipboard remains there until you either place something else there or close Windows. You can paste whatever is in the Clipboard in more than one place and in more than one document at a time.)

• **Paste Special...:** You can use this option not only to paste stuff in your document but also to link the pasted stuff to the stuff where it came from. Then, if you make a change to the stuff it was copied from, the stuff you linked gets changed too. Linking is a specialized topic that is beyond the scope of this book.

• **Select All:** A simple method of selecting all the text in your document. Alternatively, you can use a keystroke or a mouse action, but you can always use the menu option here as well.

• **Find...:** Shows the Find dialog box, in which you can search for text strings or even formatting to move quickly to a place in your document.

• **Replace...:** Enables you to replace text and formatting with other text and formatting. This powerful tool is under utilized by most users. (You have to be careful with this option. If you want to globally replace the word *form* with *document*, for example, and you forget to check the Match Whole Word Only option, you replace the text string *form* wherever it appears: FORMer, inFORMation, FORMal, reFORM, and so on. Of course, if you catch the error, you can always undo it if you haven't done anything else in the meantime.)

• **Go to...:** Opens the GoTo dialog box. You can type a number and go to that page number, for example.

• **Glossary...:** Another powerful tool more ignored than under-stood, yet very simple. A glossary entry in Word for Windows is simply any text you have highlighted, from a character to pages of information. After you highlight the text, you can save it as a glossary item by giving it a glossary name (a sort of code name). Later, when you want that text to appear in your document, you type the glossary name (the code name) you gave it and then press F3. Presto! The text appears in its entirety. Give it a try.

- **Links...:** Has to do with updating and changing links to other documents. You can link information from one document to another, which means that you can update that information by going to the source document and making the change there. The change also occurs in any linked documents.

- **Object...:** Objects in Windows are graphics, tables, text, charts, and other stuff you create in one application and store in a different application. So, in Word for Windows, an object is something you created in a different application (Excel or WordArt, for example) and then pasted into the Word for Windows document by using Paste Special to create a link. (Heavy stuff, eh?)

The View Menu

Part I discusses the different views you can have of your document on-screen. The following list explains each of the View menu options.

- **Normal:** Enables you to see your document in normal view.

- **Outline:** Enables you to see an outline view of your document. This highly specialized view is appropriate for large, complex documents that use a table of contents.

- **Page Layout:** Enables you to see your document in page layout view.

- **Draft:** Puts your document in draft mode. The quickest (but least accurate) view.

- **Toolbar:** Toggles the toolbar on and off.

- **Ribbon:** Toggles the ribbon on and off.

- **Ruler:** Toggles the ruler on and off.

- **Header/Footer...:** Displays a dialog box in which you can make choices about your headers and footers. The dialog box then opens the header/footer pane (if you are in normal view), where you can create or modify the header or footer.

- **Footnotes:** Displays a footnote pane (if you are in normal view and if you have footnotes in your document) so that you can view and modify the footnotes.

- **Annotations:** Displays an annotation pane (if you are in normal view and if you have annotations in your document) so that you can view and modify the annotations.

- **Field Codes:** These codes insert dynamic information in your document, such as dates and page numbers. You can view either the date or page number, or you can view the code itself. Clicking on this option shows the code.

- **Zoom...:** Enables you to change the magnification of the current document from 25 to 200 percent.

The Insert menu

The following list explains each of the options available on the Insert menu.

- **Break...:** Displays a dialog box in which you can choose to insert a page break, a section break, or a column break. (Column breaks are inserted only in newspaper-style columns, also known as "snaking" columns.)

- **Page Numbers...:** Displays a dialog box in which you can choose to insert the page numbers at the top or bottom of the page and whether they are left-, center-, or right-aligned.

- **Footnote...:** Displays a dialog box in which you can make choices about the footnote you want to insert. When the dialog box closes, it opens a footnote pane (if you are in normal view), where you can begin creating your footnote.

- **Bookmark...:** Displays a dialog box in which you can create a bookmark. Bookmarks in Word for Windows work just like bookmarks in real life: They act as placeholders. A bookmark can be a place in the document, or you can highlight text and give the selected text a bookmark name. (**Note:** Using book-marks is an easy way to move around in your document.)

- **Annotation...:** Opens the Annotation pane and automatically inserts the user's initials. Users then can enter comments about the document without making changes.

- **Date and Time...:** Displays a dialog box in which you can select the date and time in the format of your choice. A pretty nifty feature.

- **Field...:** Displays a dialog box in which you can select a field to enter in your document. (**Note:** Remember that fields are codes which produce certain types of information, such as the date or page numbers. There are many fields in Word for Windows, but most of us live long lives without having to deal with fields other than date and page fields.)

- **Symbol...:** One of the program's more interesting features. Displays a dialog box full of different symbols not available from the keyboard. You can change fonts in the dialog box to see more and different symbols. Most users love this feature.

- **Index Entry...:** For those who want or want to create an index for their document. There are two parts to creating an index: entering the index fields and creating the index from the entered fields. You use this option to enter the index field. If you create an index in your document, you continually use this option. After all, how many indexes do you see with only three or four entries?

- **Index...:** After you have entered all your index fields by using the previous option, you can create the index by using this option. Just place the insertion point at the end of your document and choose this option. Watch what happens. If it is successful, you will be thrilled. If not, you will be severely disappointed.

- **Table of Contents...:** This option enables you to create a table of contents (obviously). Like the index options, though, you have to have done some preliminary work first. If you used in your document the heading styles that come with Word for Windows, you can create a table of contents from them. If not, you can insert a bunch of those pesky fields mentioned earlier and use them to create the table of contents.

- **File...:** Yes, you can insert an entire file in your current document. If that's what you want to do, this is the menu option to use.

- **Frame:** A *frame* is a device you can use to position text and graphics in your document. First select the text or graphics and then choose Frame from the Insert menu. Word for Windows asks whether you want to switch to page layout view if you aren't in that view already, because you cannot accurately see how frames work in normal view. In page layout view, you can click and drag on the framed object to move it around. If you drop it in the middle of text, the text automatically makes room for it. This feature is difficult to use, but it's worth getting to know.

- **Picture...:** Inserts a picture (a graphic) from another file in your document. The dialog box also enables you to preview the picture before you insert it.

- **Object...:** Inserts something you create in another application. If you choose this option, a dialog box opens and shows you the applications in Windows that are available to you for this function. If you choose an application from this dialog box, that application opens and you then can begin to create whatever it is you want to create. When you close the application, the stuff you created is embedded in your Word for Windows document. Another powerful but complicated feature.

The Format Menu

On the Format menu, you can find the full range of formatting available in Word for Windows. The following list explains each of the Format menu options.

- **Character...**: Displays a dialog box that shows the full range of character formatting in Word for Windows. Remember to select the text first.

- **Paragraph...**: Displays a dialog box that shows the full range of paragraph formatting in Word for Windows. You must place the insertion point in the correct paragraph before using this option.

- **Tabs...**: Displays a dialog box in which you set custom tabs and create tab leaders.

- **Border...**: Displays a dialog box that enables you to add borders to selected text and graphics. You can also use this option to shade cells in a table, for example.

- **Language...**: Enables you to proof your document or selected portions of your document in a different language. *Proofing* means running the spell checker.

- **Style...**: Displays a dialog box in which you can create new styles or modify existing ones. You can also merge styles from other documents or templates.

- **Page Setup...**: Displays a dialog box in which you can change margins, change the size of your page, and select different paper feeders if your printer is equipped for it.

- **Columns...**: Displays a dialog box in which you can change selected text to newspaper (or snaking) columns.

- **Section Layout...**: Displays a dialog box in which you can make various choices about a particular section in your document. (See Part IV for more information about sections.)

- **Frame...**: Not available unless you first select a framed object. Displays a dialog box in which you can modify how the framed object is positioned on the page. You can also remove the frame with this option.

- **Picture...**: Not available unless you first select a picture. Displays a dialog box in which you can crop or scale the picture to make the picture match a certain size.

The Tools Menu

The following list explains all the options available from the Tools menu.

- **Spelling...:** Opens the Spell Checker dialog box. You can check the spelling of selected text or of the entire document.

- **Grammar...:** Yes, Word for Windows has its own grammar checker. In fact, using the grammar checker also gives you a spell check at the same time. Two for the price of one, so to speak. You can set various options and have the options explained in this dialog box.

- **Thesaurus:** For those unfamiliar with this nice little feature, a thesaurus lets you select a word you want to replace with a synonym. The Word for Windows thesaurus gives you this ability.

- **Hyphenation...:** Displays a dialog box in which you can make choices about hyphenating selected text or the entire document.

- **Bullets and Numbering:** Displays a dialog box in which you can select bullets or numbers for selected paragraphs. You can also make a number of choices about the bullets and numbers. This feature is rather complex but not difficult to use. See Part IV for more information about this feature.

- **Create Envelope...:** Displays a dialog box in which you can enter an address and return address for your envelope. You can also select from a number of different envelope types so that you don't have to worry about formatting. (**Hint:** If you have already created a letter with the address block, you can select the address block before selecting this option and you don't even have to enter the address.)

- **Revision Marks...:** Revision marks are used mostly in law firms, but others can use them. When you use revision marks, text proposed to be deleted is formatted as strikethrough (~~to be deleted~~, for example). You can choose formatting options for proposed new text. Also places a mark next to any paragraph with text to be deleted or added.

- **Compare Versions...:** Enables you to compare the current document with another document you choose. This option opens a dialog box in which you can select the other document. Differences are formatted according to choices made in the Revision Marks dialog box.

- **Sorting...:** Enables you to sort selected paragraphs alphabetically or numerically, whichever is appropriate. Remember that a paragraph can be any amount of text. You create a paragraph by pressing Enter.

- **Calculate:** Calculates selected numbers. The numbers can be in a table or in a sentence. This option follows the usual rules of arithmetic (numbers in parentheses are treated as negative numbers, for example). The result is placed in the Clipboard and appears briefly in the status bar. Because the result is in the Clipboard, you can paste it anywhere in your document.

- **Repaginate Now:** Immediately causes Word for Windows to repaginate the current document. Used when page breaks are inserted.

- **Record Macro...:** Turns on the macro recorder. Macros are small programs that can range from quite simple to quite complex. Writing a macro (as opposed to recording one) requires at least some understanding of programming. A discussion of this advanced feature is beyond the scope of this book.

- **Macro...:** Enables you to edit previously created macros or to create new macros without using the recorder. You can also delete macros by using this option.

- **Options...:** Displays a dialog box in which you can set various options in Word for Windows. Some options include viewing options, saving options, spelling options, and printing options.

The Table menu

The table feature in Word for Windows is probably one of its best features. You can use tables to set up financial tables and to arrange paragraphs side-by-side. Part V discusses the table feature in depth.

The Table menu changes dynamically to reflect your current activity, so don't be alarmed if you notice that the Table menu contains choices it didn't contain the last time you used it. You cannot insert a table within a table, for example, so if the insertion point is in a table when you open the Table menu, you get different choices than if the insertion point is not currently in a table.

The following list explains the options that are available when you are working in a table. Otherwise, most of the options under the Table menu are not available. Although the first option (Insert Table) is available only when you are *not* currently in a table, however, it is shown in order to describe how to begin constructing a table. Got all that?

- **Insert Table...:** Displays a dialog box in which you can choose the number of columns and rows you want your table to have. (If the insertion point is in a table, this option is Insert Cells... instead.)

- **Delete Cells...**: Enables you to delete selected cells in a table. Displays a dialog box so that you can tell Word for Windows how to handle the remaining cells.

- **Merge Cells:** Enables you to merge selected cells. (**Note:** You cannot merge cells that have already been merged.)

- **Convert Text to Table...**: Enables you to select existing text and place it in a table. (**Note:** If you are already in a table, this option changes to Convert Table to Text and opens a dialog box in which you can indicate how you want this done.)

- **Select Row:** Selects the entire row in which the insertion point is placed.

- **Select Column:** Selects the entire column in which the insertion point is placed.

- **Select Table:** Selects the entire table.

- **Row Height...**: Displays a dialog box in which you can make choices about the height of the selected row (or rows). You can also indent the table and center or right-align it. (Now here's a poorly placed choice: If you want to center your table, you must choose Row Height. Guess Microsoft ran out of choices here.)

- **Column Width...**: Displays a dialog box in which you can enter the width of the selected column (or columns).

- **Split Table:** Enters a return directly above the row the insertion point is in, thereby splitting the table in two. Also enters a return directly above the table if it is the first item in your document.

- **Gridlines:** A toggle option that is turned on if you select it. If you select it again, you turn it off. You can tell when it's on by the checkmark next to it. Turning Gridlines on causes the table gridlines to be displayed on-screen. (**Note:** This is different from formatting the gridlines. You format the gridlines if you want them to print. Whether they show in your document has no effect on printing them unless they are also formatted.)

The Window menu

The following list explains the options available from the Window menu.

- **New Window:** Opens a new window on the current document.

- **Arrange All:** Arranges all open windows on the screen.

- **Numbered windows:** Shows all open windows. Each window has a number in front of it. Click on the number to open the window you want.

The Help menu

Help contains the equivalent of an on-line manual with many ways to find the topic that interests you. You can also print the various help topics and create a kind of mini-manual. Help also has two tutorials, product-support questions and answers and phone numbers, and a special help section for WordPerfect users. I urge you to play with the help features until you become familiar with them. You will be glad you did for as long as you use Word for Windows. The following list explains each of the options on the Help menu.

- **Help Index:** Opens the Help window. You can use this window to choose various topics. You can also print any help topic from this window. (**Hint:** Notice the button that says Instructions. If you click that button, a window opens that contains instructions about how to use Help.)

- **Getting Started:** The first of a two-part tutorial that gives you enough information about how Word for Windows works so that you can begin working almost immediately. It's even kind of fun to take. Really!

- **Learning Word:** The second, more comprehensive part of the two-part tutorial. If you don't understand a certain feature, try using this tutorial. It may make things more clear to you.

- **Product Support:** Opens a window that contains answers to the most common questions and also telephone numbers you can call if all else fails.

- **Word Perfect Help:** For WordPerfect users. This option shows you how to do in Word for Windows what you already know how to do in WordPerfect. Ex-WordPerfect users rate this feature highly.

- **About...:** Displays a dialog box that tells you almost nothing you care about.

The Toolbar

The first part of this part (huh?) took a long look at the menus in Word for Windows. If you determine that you will use only the menus, you don't even have to look at this section. The toolbar is nothing more than a collection of buttons (tools) that perform some of the same functions as the menus.

The difference is that using the toolbar is much quicker in most instances. (Using the toolbar requires a mouse.) If you use the menus often, you may find yourself muttering that there ought to be a quicker and easier way. There are better ways, in some cases. The toolbar is one of those cases.

This is not to say that you will find every tool on the toolbar to be all that useful. Like most of us, you probably will use some of the tools (or buttons, if you insist) quite a bit and some hardly at all. So, just use the ones you like, and don't bother with the others.

You can toggle the toolbar on and off by choosing it from the View menu.

As you can see in the following figure, there are 22 icons. Each icon is discussed in this list.

- **File New:** Shows a new file based on the normal template. If you want to use a different template, you must use the File New menu option instead.

- **File Open:** Shows the File Open dialog box.

- **File Save:** Opens the File Save dialog box for new documents; saves changes made to existing documents without opening a dialog box.

- **Edit Cut:** Cuts (removes) the selection to the Clipboard. (Remember the Clipboard?)

- **Edit Copy:** Copies the selection to the Clipboard.

- **Edit Paste:** Pastes the Clipboard contents into the document wherever the insertion point is located.

- **Edit Undo:** Undoes your last action. Easily the most important button on the toolbar.

- **Insert Number/Create Hanging Indent:** Now, here is a nice tool. All you have to do is select one or more paragraphs and click once on this button. Voila! The selected paragraphs are numbered in order and are properly indented.

To change the starting number of your paragraphs or to change the numbering styles, choose Bullets and Numbering from the Tools menu. The Numbering part of this dialog box will open.

- **Insert Bullet/Create Hanging Indent:** This tool works the same way as the preceding tool, except that you use this tool to insert bullets rather than numbers. To see a variety of alternatives to the bullet character, double click directly on the bullet.

You can select other bullets by choosing Bullets and Numbering from the Tools menu. The Bullets part of this dialog box opens. (**Note:** The alternatives to the bullet character are limited by your installed fonts. To produce a bullet, the symbol font must be installed. To produce other characters, fonts such as Zapf Dingbats must be installed.)

- **Unindent:** Removes full indents. Notice the arrow pointing to the left. (What? You can't see the arrow? Better have your eyes checked.)

- **Indent:** Indents selected paragraphs according to default tab stops. Again, notice the arrow pointing to the right. If you can't discern the arrow, refer to the preceding item.

- **Insert Table:** Starts a grid that allows you to use your mouse to select numbers of rows and columns. You might have to play with this grid once or twice before you get the hang of it.

- **Format Columns:** Opens a graphic box that enables you to use the mouse to select as many as six snaking (newspaper style) columns. The problem with this tool is that it applies to the entire document, not just to selected text. If you want only some of your text to be formatted in columns, choose Columns from the Format menu.

- **Insert Frame:** This button places a frame around selected text or objects. Frames are used in Word for Windows to enable you to position the framed object anywhere on the page by dragging it.

- **Insert Drawing:** Opens Microsoft Draw, one of the applets included with Word for Windows. Graphics can be created in Draw and embedded in your document. Draw is similar to Paintbrush.

- **Insert Graph:** Opens Microsoft Graph, another new applet. You can use this applet to create graphs based on figures in a table.

- **Create Envelope:** Opens a dialog box in which you can enter an address and a return address. The address can be pasted in from the letter, assuming that you have already created the letter.

- **Spell Checker:** Invokes the spell checker.

- **File Print Default:** Prints the active document in its entirety without generating a dialog box. If you want to print selected pages, you must use the File Print menu.

- **View Zoom Whole Page:** One of three zooming buttons; shrinks the document to a smaller percentage so that you can view the entire page. The document is still fully interactive and editable. (But try editing it.)

- **View Zoom 100:** Shows the active document at 100 percent viewing size.

- **View Zoom Page Width:** One of the nicer tools; adjusts the size of the document so that it fits on the screen, relieving you of having to scroll horizontally. Keep two things in mind, though: Sometimes it doesn't fit the entire document to the screen, which means that you can use the View Zoom menu to adjust the magnification, and if your margins are the type that the document is naturally smaller than your screen, this button enlarges the magnification. So there.

The Ribbon

The ribbon is similar to the toolbar in that it provides shortcuts to using the menus. There is nothing on the ribbon you cannot do by using the menus. If you, like the rest of us, however, are continually looking for shortcuts in your work, you will appreciate the ribbon.

The ribbon is different from the toolbar in one significant way: Most of the items on the ribbon are either character- or paragraph-formatting shortcuts. To use the ribbon, select whatever it is you want to work on and then click on the appropriate part of the ribbon (see the following figure).

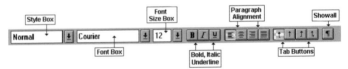

 You can toggle the ribbon on and off by choosing it from the <u>V</u>iew menu.

 You can use the ribbon to quickly check certain formatting characteristics for selected text. That is, if you're not sure about the font or font size for certain text, just select it and glance at the ribbon.

 If you select text and glance at the ribbon only to see a blank box, it just means that you selected text that has varied formats. If you want to check the font size of some text and the font size box is blank, for example, the selected text contains different font sizes.

 The first three features on the ribbon (style box, font box, and font size box) each have a down arrow to the right. Clicking on the down arrow displays a list of available choices. You don't have to use the lists, however; you can just type your choice in the box if you are sure that the choice exists. It is sometimes a little quicker, for example, to type the font size than it is to click on the down arrow and then choose the size from the list. The following list explains the features on the ribbon.

 • **Style box:** Enables you to create and apply styles to selected paragraphs. This feature is one of the few on the ribbon that applies to paragraphs (as do all styles) rather than to selected text. Notice the down arrow to the right of the style box. (**Note:** See Part IV for more information about styles.)

- **Font box:** Enables you to apply to selected text any previously installed font. This is a nice, easy method of changing fonts.

- **Font size box:** Enables you to quickly change the font size for selected text.

- **Bold, italic, underline buttons:** These buttons make life easier for you. Select the text and click the appropriate button — that's all there is to it. To remove the formatting, select the button again.

- **Paragraph alignment:** Enables you to align selected paragraphs as you choose: left (the default), centered, right, and justified. If you look closely, you can even see that the lines on the buttons indicate the particular alignment.

- **Show all:** Enables you to toggle between displaying and not displaying nonprinting characters. If you like to see your paragraph and tab symbols and the spaces between words, you can click this button on. It is a toggle, so you can display or not display as you choose.

The Ruler

The ruler is more complex than either the toolbar or the ribbon. For one thing, the ruler has more than one view (two views normally, and a third if you are working in tables). The different views of the ruler are called *scales.* The default view, or scale, is indent. You can change the ruler to margin scale, and, if you are in a table, the ruler can also be displayed in table scale. The following figure shows the ruler in indent scale.

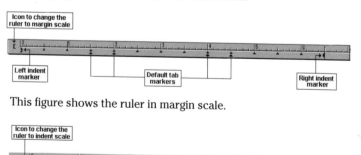

This figure shows the ruler in margin scale.

The following figure shows the ruler in table scale.

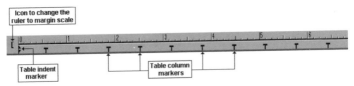

No matter which scale is displayed, there is nothing you can do with the ruler that you cannot do from the menus.

Using indents versus margins

Many newcomers to Word for Windows are confused by the issue of indenting versus changing the margins. Contributing to this confusion is the fact that every word-processing system treats this topic differently. But, because this is a book about Word for Windows, it behooves you to look into the way Word for Windows handles this issue.

In Word for Windows, indentation is *paragraph specific*. That means, if you want to make a paragraph or a group of paragraphs wider or narrower, you don't change the margin. Instead, you change the indents for the selected paragraphs.

Margins, on the other hand, can be either document specific or page specific, at your option. When you change the margins, therefore, you change them for the entire document (or for the page, if you prefer), but not for selected paragraphs. If you want to change the margins for a page, you have to think about section breaks.

See Part IV for more information about sections.

Most Word for Windows users find it easier to leave the margins at the default setting and forget about them. If you want to adjust portions of your document to gain space or to fill spots, you can use indentation instead. (Naturally, there may be times you want to change the margins on a specific page. You cannot do it from the ruler, though.)

You can change the indentation settings for selected paragraphs by using the ruler when it is in indent scale.

You can also use the ruler to change the left and right margins when it is in margin scale, but if you use the ruler, the margins change for the entire document.

You must choose Page Setup from the Format menu to change the margins for a selected page.

Using the ruler to indent

When the ruler is in indent scale, you can use the icons and markers on the ruler to indent selected paragraphs.

1. Select the paragraph (or paragraphs) and then just slide the indent markers along the ruler by clicking and dragging.

2. If you slide the markers toward the center of the page, you increase the indent (you cause the text to move farther away from the edges of the page).

3. If you slide the markers away from the center, you add a negative indent. One of the nicer features of Word for Windows is that you can print selected paragraphs outside the margins.

You may have noticed that the left marker is different from the right one. The reason is that there are three types of left indents in Word for Windows, and you can use any of them by using that left indent marker. This list shows the three types of indents:

• **Full indent:** Each line of the paragraph is indented.

• **First-line indent:** Only the first line of the paragraph is indented (many users prefer to simply press Tab).

• **Hanging indent:** The first line of the paragraph extends to the left of the rest of the lines; used most commonly with bullets and numbers.

Setting a left indent

1. Select the paragraph (or paragraphs).

2. If you want a full indent, be sure to place the mouse pointer on the bottom part of the indent marker. Then just drag the marker toward the center of the page. Both parts come with you.

3. If you want a first-line indent, be sure to place the mouse pointer on the top part of the indent marker. Then just drag the top part toward the center of the page. Only the top part comes with you.

4. If you want a hanging indent, place the mouse pointer on the bottom part of the indent marker and then press Shift. Drag the marker toward the center of the page. It should come without the top part.

Setting a right indent

1. Select the paragraph (or paragraphs).
2. Place the mouse pointer on the right indent marker.
3. Drag the marker toward the center of the page.

Using the ruler to change margins

1. Be sure that the ruler is in margin scale. (To get to the margin scale from the indent scale, click on the margin icon on the left side of the ruler.
2. Place the mouse pointer on the left or right margin marker, as appropriate.
3. Click and drag.

When you use the ruler, you can change only the left and right margins, not the top and bottom margins. Also, using the ruler changes the margins for the entire document, not just selected paragraphs or sections.

Using the ruler with tables

You have almost no reason to use the ruler with tables. Anything you want to do with tables can be done from either the table itself or from the Table menu. See Part V for more information about tables.

Double-clicking on the Indent Icon or the Margin Icon on the left side of the ruler displays the Paragraph dialog box, in which you can make more choices about custom settings.

Part III
File Management in Word for Windows

You can use the File menu to handle all your file needs in Word for Windows (another clever design decision by the friendly folks at Microsoft). File handling in Word for Windows can be summed up as follows:

- Create a new file by choosing New
- Retrieve an existing file by choosing Open
- Save a new file by using Save or Save As
- Save an existing file with a new name by using Save As
- Close an active file by using Close
- Locate a file by using Find File

In this part, you learn how to use these steps to handle your files in Word for Windows.

Creating Files

1. Choose New from the File menu. This step opens the File New dialog box.

2. Unless you want to use a special template, just click the OK button. Your new file is based on the Normal template.

Click the first button on the toolbar to get the same result.

Don't choose Template in the New box unless you really want to create a template. (You learn more about templates later in this part.)

Saving Files

One of the basic truths in word processing is that you cannot save your work too often. If you have ever lost work because you did not save it regularly, you know how accurate this statement is. On the positive side, if you attempt to close Word for Windows without having saved your work, the program prompts you for each file involved. To learn more about saving files, see Chapter 15 in *Word for Windows For Dummies*.

Saving a file for the first time

1. Choose Save or Save As from the File menu. When you save a file for the first time, these two options work in exactly the same way. This step opens the File Save As dialog box.

Press Alt+Shift+F2 (Save) or Alt+F2 (Save As) instead of using the menu, or click the third button in the toolbar. This step works as Save As when you save a file the first time.

2. Type the filename in the File Name box.

You don't have to bother adding an extension unless you want to use something other than the Word for Windows default extension: .DOC (short for *doc*ument). Unless you have a compelling reason to use a different extension, it is easier to let Word for Windows automatically add the default extension.

3. Select the correct drive and directory if they are not already selected.

4. Click the OK button. (If a Summary Information dialog box appears, see the section "Finding Files" later in this part.)

Saving an existing file

TIP

Choose Save from the File menu. That's it.

Rather than use the menu, just click once on the third button from the left on the toolbar.

An *existing file* is a file that has already been saved at least once, so it already has a filename and a home (drive and directory). For this reason, there is no need to enter any more information about the file; saving it just means updating it.

Saving an existing file with a new name

1. Choose Save As from the File menu (or press Alt+F2) to open the File Save As dialog box.

2. At this point, the procedure is exactly the same as saving a file for the first time, so give the file a name and be sure that you have selected the proper drive and directory.

What's going on here? Why would you want to save a file with a new name? The most common reason is that you have a file that has to be modified, but you also want to keep the original version. This procedure is designed for this situation. Also, you choose File Save As to save to the A or B drive to make that extra disk for backups.

TIP

When you do this, the original file no longer remains open. Word for Windows stores it back in its directory in its original state (as long as you haven't saved any changes while it was open). You can use this capability to your advantage. Suppose that you have been working for a couple of hours on a large file and you think that you have screwed up the file beyond hope. As long as you haven't saved your changes, you can choose File Save As. The original file remains unchanged. On-screen, the new file is in its screwed-up state. You can continue to work on it and hope that you can fix it before your boss comes along, or you can retrieve the original file and try again.

Saving files with the autosave feature

The Word for Windows autosave feature has caused some confusion even to experienced users of the program. (Yes, even experienced users can get confused.)

Unlike WordPerfect's autosave feature (and unlike the autosave feature in the previous version of Word for Windows), the autosave feature in this version does not perform a save operation when it automatically saves documents. (Tell me that *that's* not confusing!)

The autosave feature probably should have been called the disaster-prevention feature because that's the service it performs. Word for Windows creates a temporary file (called a temp file) as you work. That's where it stores all the changes you make. Every time you save your file, you clear the temp file; this is true for every document you have open.

Then, at the end of your session, when you close Word for Windows, the temp file gets erased.

If you do not exit Word for Windows normally, however (when you turn off your machine without thinking or have a power failure, for example), the program keeps the temp file. Then, the next time you open Word for Windows, whatever you had in the temp file immediately appears on-screen. The title bar displays (RECOVERED) after the filename. It does this with multiple files and with files you didn't even save in the first place.

The catch (there's a catch, of course — this is real life) is that the autosave feature must be turned on, *and* enough time must have passed for it to have performed an autosave. In other words, if you set the autosave option for 15 minutes and a power failure occurs 8 minutes later, Word for Windows will not have autosaved anything because 15 minutes didn't pass. Get it? Another way of looking at this is that, if you set autosave for 15 minutes, you cannot lose more than 15 minutes worth of work (and that's a worst-case scenario).

The nice thing about this feature is that, if you decide for whatever reason that you didn't want to save your changes, you still have that option, even after the recovery. This is another way of saying that you still must save your recovered files when you open Word for Windows again.

The other catch (yep — another one) is that, unfortunately, the autosave feature is not turned on automatically when Word for Windows is installed. You have to turn it on. See Chapter 28 in *Word for Windows For Dummies* for more on autosaves.

Turning on the autosave feature

1. Choose Options from the Tools menu to open the Options dialog box.

2. In the Category box on the left, choose Save. If you don't see it, use the vertical scroll bar to find it (See the following figure).

3. Click on the Automatic Save Every line to place an X in the box. Most users prefer ten minutes, but you can use the up and down arrows to scroll to any setting you want. (You may find that a setting of less than ten minutes becomes sort of irritating because Word for Windows stops processing during the autosave operation.)

4. Click the OK button. That's it. Now your Autosave feature is turned on.

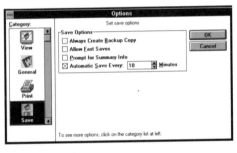

Using autosave

Actually, you really don't want to use the autosave feature. It's like insurance: Ya gotta have it, but you really don't want to use it. It is instructive, however, to see how it works. Try the following test:

1. Be sure that only Word for Windows is running. (You realize, of course, that Windows *must* be running, so that's OK.)

1. Set autosave to 1 or 2 minutes and click on OK.

2. Create a new document. Be sure that it is the only document you have open.

3. Type some random text. Be sure that you wait at least two minutes so that the autosave feature has a chance to work.

4. Reboot your computer. (Oh, go ahead. It won't hurt anything. Really.)

5. Open Windows and then open Word for Windows. Your test document should appear on-screen with the word (RECOVERED) in the title bar.

Opening Files

Opening a file, of course, means that you are retrieving an existing file.

 When you open a file in Word for Windows, the File Open dialog box has an option called Read Only. If you check this box when you open the file, neither you nor anyone else can make changes to the file (which may be a blessing in disguise).

Opening a file created in Word for Windows

1. Choose Open from the File menu or press Ctrl+F12. This step opens the File Open dialog box. Look familiar? It should. It's the other side of the coin, so to speak, of the File Save As dialog box.

 Rather than use the File menu, click once on the second button from the left on the toolbar (the one that's cleverly disguised as a file folder that is opening).

2. Be sure that you are in the correct directory on the correct drive. If so, the file you want should be listed on the left. If it isn't listed, the problem may be that the file has a different filename extension (something other than .DOC). Word for Windows uses this filename extension by default.

3. You can change that setting by clicking on the down arrow to the right of List Files of Type, located at the bottom of the dialog box. You can select All Files from the list. If your file still doesn't appear, you are probably in the wrong directory.

Opening a file not created in Word for Windows

 The procedure for opening a file not created in Word for Windows is amazingly simple. It is exactly the same procedure for opening a Word for Windows file. The only difference is that the program recognizes that it isn't a Word for Windows file and makes an attempt to convert it. This procedure opens the Convert File dialog box: All you have to do is click on OK. For more help, see Chapter 16, "Other Documents — Alien and ASCII," in *Word for Windows For Dummies*.

You may not be able to convert some files because the Word for
Windows files that are necessary to convert them may not have
been installed. You don't do anything in this case unless you want
to install those files now. If you do, you can run the Word for
Windows Setup program again. Consult your Word for Windows
documentation for help.

Finding Files

Finding files means pretty much what you think it means. If you
cannot remember the filename of that file you created eight
months ago and you cannot remember where you put it, Word for
Windows provides a couple of features to help you: Summary
Information and Find File.

To use File Find, follow these steps:

1. Choose Find File from the File menu to open the Find File
   dialog box (See the next figure).

2. You can select more than one file at a time from the list of files
   by pressing Ctrl while you select each additional file.

3. Choose from the buttons at the bottom to perform the operation you want. You can open, copy, print, or delete the files you
   selected. This feature can be a real time-saver. The Summary
   button displays summary information (see the following
   section) for the selected file, and the Options button lets you
   choose which information about the file you want to see.

![Find File dialog box screenshot showing paths searched, file name list, and content preview of MS DRAW documentation, with buttons Open, Print, Summary, Search, Preview, Delete, Copy, Options, Close, and Open as Read Only checkbox]

To change drives or directories, click the Search button to open the Search dialog box. If it looks familiar, that is because it is similar to the Summary Information dialog box. Enter any information you remember about the file you want to retrieve.

There are three ways to change the path. (Remember that the path is a list of drives and directories. In this case, you want to list all the drives and directories in which you think that the file might be located.)

1. Click on the down arrow to the right of the Drives box to see a list of places to search.
2. If you know the exact path, type it directly in the Path box.
3. Click the Edit Path button to open the Edit Path dialog box.

In the Find File dialog box, you can browse through the drive and directory structure on your computer. You can add and delete drives and directories from the search path. When you have completed building the search path, click the OK button.

Summary information: What the heck Is this?

When you save a file for the first time, after you give it a name and select a drive and directory for it, you probably will see the Summary Info dialog box. In this dialog box, you can enter identifying data about the current file. You can search on that data later by using File Find File.

You can cause the Summary Info dialog box not to appear automatically by choosing Options from the Tools menu to open the Options dialog box. In the Category box on the left, choose Save and then clear the check box next to Prompt for Summary Info. (You can open the Summary Info dialog box at any time for an active file by choosing Summary Info from the File menu.)

The Summary Info dialog box is a great feature to help you locate your files. (What? You have never in your life lost a file?) You can also use it to print, copy, delete, or open one or more than one file at a time.

Using Templates

When you create a file, you usually start with a blank screen and then type the information that will become part of the file. This method is fine most of the time. But haven't you sometimes created files that were very similar to other files you might have created in the past? One example might be a memo. You don't mind typing the memo, but you think, "Jeez, wouldn't it be nice if I didn't have to type all that stuff on top every time?"

That's why templates were designed. So, rather than type all that stuff at the top of the memo every time, when you begin your new file, just choose the Memo template and all that stuff already will be there. You can just begin typing the body of the memo.

All files in Word for Windows are based on a template. The default template is the Normal template which is what most people use almost exclusively. This template contains only the most basic settings, such as the default font, font size, margins, and line spacing. You can modify any of these settings, of course, either in a particular document or in the template. If you change the Normal template, all new documents based on it have the new settings.

If you change the Normal template, although all new files based on it reflect the new settings, the old documents are unaffected. You have to change their settings individually because they already have been saved.

Word for Windows comes with a set of templates designed at the factory, so to speak. You can use these templates and modify them to suit yourself. In addition to these templates, you can create your own. Templates can contain glossary entries, boilerplate text, styles, macros, and customized menus and toolbar buttons. (Highly specialized templates can be complex to create and may require the services of a Word for Windows expert.)

One more thing. Macros and glossaries can be template specific. That is, you can assign new macros and glossaries to a specific template so that they are available with only that template, or you can make them globally available.

If you don't get templates, see Chapter 13 in *Word for Windows For Dummies*.

Creating a template

There are three methods for creating new templates: by using File New (from scratch), an existing template, and a new template from an existing document.

Creating a new template by using File New

1. Choose New from the File menu to open the File New dialog box.

You *must* use File New to create a new template from scratch. The File New dialog box is the only place you can select a new template in Word for Windows.

2. Click on Template in the New box. A new file appears, but rather than Document 1, it says Template 1.

3. Type the text you want in the template. Customize it in any way you want.

4. Save the template as you would save any file. Word for Windows automatically adds the .DOT extension. The new template should appear in the template list when you create a new file.

Creating a template from an existing template

1. Choose Open from the File menu or click the second button from the left on the toolbar to open the File Open dialog box.

2. At the bottom of the dialog box, under List Files of Type, click once on the down arrow to the right. Choose Document Templates.

   If no files show up in the File Name box, you are probably not in the correct directory. Template files usually are stored in the WINWORD directory, so be sure that you are in that directory.

3. Select the template file you want. When it opens, make the changes you want.

4. When you have finished, choose Save As from the File menu. Give the template file a new name. Because you began this process with a template, there is no need to change directories or worry about the file extension.

5. Finally, choose Close from the File menu. Your new template should appear in the list of templates when you use File New.

Creating a template from an existing document file

1. Choose New from the File menu.

2. Choose the Template option in the New box.

3. In the Use Template box (where it probably says NORMAL), type the filename of the file on which you want to base the new template. If the file is on a different drive or in a different directory, you have to include them (D:\DOCFILES\TESTFILE.DOC, for example).

4. When the file opens, make any changes you want. Remember that, if text is in the file, that text appears in every new document based on that template.

5. Choose <u>S</u>ave from the <u>F</u>ile menu and give your new template a filename. Remember that Word for Windows automatically adds the .DOT extension.

Using a template

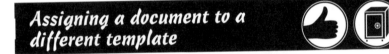

1. Choose <u>N</u>ew from the <u>F</u>ile menu to open the File New dialog box.

2. Select the template you want to use.

3. Click the OK button or press Return. That's it.

To see how templates work, try using the FAX template that comes with Word for Windows.

Assigning a document to a different template

1. Be sure that the document in question is the active document.

2. Choose <u>T</u>emplate from the <u>F</u>ile menu to open the Template dialog box.

3. Click on the down arrow to the right of the Attach <u>D</u>ocument To box.

4. Choose the template to which you want to attach the current document.

5. Select the way you want to store new macros and glossaries. It's best to select <u>P</u>rompt for Each New if it isn't already selected.

Part IV
Formatting in Word for Windows

Formatting a document in any word-processing system is usually the meat and potatoes of that system. If the system doesn't provide enough formatting tools, or if formatting is difficult, people just don't want to use that system.

Fortunately, Word for Windows provides superior formatting tools and many ways to use them. If you must make a negative comment (and who doesn't, from time to time?), it probably would be that there are so many ways to format, it takes time to learn them all.

Guess what? You don't have to learn them all. In fact, it's necessary to learn just one way. As you become more proficient with Word for Windows, you can begin exploring the alternative methods for different formatting tasks. The best way for someone new to the program is to use the menus. Remember that the menus give you access to all the Word for Windows features and that — if you cannot remember that nifty shortcut method — you can always resort to using the menus.

Thankfully, most of the formatting options in Word for Windows are found on the Format menu. Even with the one major exception, tables, it depends on what you want to format. Some formatting options depend on other actions — you cannot format a frame or a picture, for example, unless you first insert one in your document and then select it.

Speaking of selecting, don't forget that you must select whatever it is you want to format before you begin formatting.

Although Word for Windows has a number of formatting options, there are really only four general categories:

- Character formatting
- Paragraph formatting
- Section and document formatting
- Other formatting

The following table shows all the formatting options in Word for Windows and with which category of formatting they are associated. Many of the options indicate shortcut approaches, which can be real time-savers. To see the full range of formats available for a formatting task, use the menus.

Format	Category	Use
Character	Character	You can change the appearance of selected text by using character formatting, including bolding, italicizing, underlining, changing the font and font sizes, and more.
		Use the ribbon or the Format Character menu.
Border	Paragraph	You can add a variety of border types around the selected text, graphic, or table.
		Use the Format Border menu.
Frame	Paragraph	Frames are used to position selected text and graphics on the page. This advanced topic is not covered in this book.

Format	Category	Use
		Add a frame by using the Insert Frame menu or the toolbar. Format an existing frame by using Format Frame.
Language	Other	Use this option to spell-check selected text in the language of your choice.
		Use the Format Paragraph menu.
Page Setup	Document/Section	This option is used to change margins, page size, page orientation (portrait or landscape), and more.
		Use the Format Page Setup menu. No shortcuts for this option.
Paragraph	Paragraph	Paragraph formatting includes indentation, space above and below selected paragraphs, line spacing, paragraph orientation, and paragraph and pagination choices.
		Use the toolbar, ribbon, ruler, or Format Paragraph menu.
Picture	Paragraph	You can crop and scale pictures in your document (but only if you have a picture in your document and select it first).
		Use Format Picture.
Section	Document/Section	A *section break* is an artificial break within a document (it doesn't print). Section breaks are necessary for changing headers and footers in a document, snaking (newspaper style) columns, footnote placement and sequencing, changing margins, and page orientation.

Format	Category	Use
		Insert a section break from the Insert Break menu. Use Format Section Layout to format a section.
Tabs	Paragraph	Word for Windows has four types of tabs: left, center, right, and decimal, in addition to the default tab stops. There are also three types of tab leaders.
		Use the ribbon, the ruler, or the Format Tabs menu.
Tables	Other	*Tables* are gridlike structures you can use to create financial columns and side-by-side paragraphs. You can insert and delete rows and columns as well as individual cells. You also can determine row height and column width and whether the gridlines show.
		Use the Table menu in addition to a variety of other formatting options, which are described in this table. To print gridlines, for example, select the table and use Format Border. Or, to add space in rows, use Format Paragraph.

Character Formatting

Character formatting is one of the simplest tasks, and it is among the most fun. (Fun? How does a word like *fun* get into a technical-reference manual? What I like about character formatting is that your changes show up immediately on-screen. This capability always gets "oohs" and "aahs" from people in the DOS crowd who are new to Windows.) You can get more character formatting details in Chapter 9 of *Word for Windows For Dummies*.

Using the dialog box to apply character formatting

1. Select the text you want to format.
2. Choose Character from the Format menu to open the Format Character dialog box.
3. Choose the formatting options you want.
4. Click on OK.

The Format Character dialog box contains all the character-formatting options Word for Windows offers. Some of the options have shortcuts, but others don't. If you want to superscript a number, for example, or add spacing between letters in a word, you can find those options in this dialog box (see the next figure).

TIP To get a feel for all the options here, select some random text and try the different options to see the effect. That's the easiest and best way to become familiar with all the options.

Using the ribbon to apply character formatting

1. Select the text you want to format.
2. Select the appropriate button on the ribbon. From the ribbon, you can change the font and font size, and make text bold-faced, italicized, and underlined. These options are among the most frequently used options, so the ribbon is pretty useful.

Character-formatting keyboard shortcuts

Some of the keyboard shortcuts are almost obvious: Ctrl+B for bold, Ctrl+I for indent, and Ctrl+U for underline, for example. Some are not so obvious, though. You can display a listing of character-formatting keystrokes (and many others) from the Help menu.

1. Choose Help Index from the Help menu.
2. In the Index window, choose Keyboard and Mouse.

3. In the Keyboard and Mouse window, choose Character Formatting Key Combinations.

4. To print the listing, choose Print Topic from the File menu (in the Help window, not in the Word for Windows window).

Paragraph Formatting

It's time now to admit to a small lie. Every other part of this book stresses that you must select whatever it is you want to work on before you work on it. That requirement also applies to paragraphs. The small lie is that you don't have to select the entire paragraph in order for any of these formatting options to work. You simply must make sure that the insertion point is in the paragraph. (There. I admitted it, and I feel better now.)

On the other hand, if you want to apply the formats to more than one consecutive paragraph, you must select the paragraphs that are involved. (So, it wasn't much of a lie, was it?)

When you select a paragraph and format it, the rest of your document is unaffected. If you format a blank paragraph and press Enter, however, you carry that formatting forward. That's because all paragraph formatting is stored in the paragraph mark at the end of the paragraph. (This feature can lead to problems if you inadvertently delete a paragraph mark for a heavily formatted paragraph. The paragraph suddenly changes. In this case, an immediate Undo is appropriate.)

To format paragraphs, choose Format Paragraph. The Paragraph dialog box opens. (See the following figure.)

There's lots more info on paragraph formatting in Chapter 10 of *Word for Windows For Dummies*.

Paragraph		
Alignment: Left	Spacing	OK
Indentation	Before: 0 li	Cancel
From Left: 0"	After: 1 li	Tabs...
From Right: 0"	Line Spacing: At:	
First Line: 0"	Exactly 1 li	
Pagination	Sample	
☐ Page Break Before		
☐ Keep With Next		
☐ Keep Lines Together		
Line Numbers		
☐ Suppress		

Paragraph alignment

1. Click on the down arrow to the right of the Alignment box to see the alignment choices, and click on the alignment you want.

2. Alternatively, click the alignment button of your choice on the ribbon.

TIP You can also press Ctrl+L for left alignment; Ctrl+R for right alignment; Ctrl+J for justify; and Ctrl+E for center alignment. (Ctrl+E? Are they *kidding*? Why would Microsoft choose E rather than C for center? Because, in its infinite wisdom, it decided to use Ctrl+C as a keystroke to copy selected text to the Clipboard.)

Indentation

Left indentation

1. For a full indent from the left, increase the number in the From Left box under Indentation. Notice that the sample reflects your settings.

2. You can also click to enter negative numbers in any of these indentation boxes. Word for Windows prints selected paragraphs outside the margin, which is another reason not to mess with your margins.

Right indentation

The same instructions you use for left indentation apply here.

First-line indentation

You can indent just the first line by using the first-line setting. The alternative is to press Tab on the keyboard. The choice is yours.

Hanging indents

In a *hanging indent,* the first line of the paragraph extends to the left of the rest of the lines in the paragraph. It's used most commonly with numbers and bullets.

1. To create a hanging indent, increase the number in the From Left box.

2. Decrease the number by the same amount in the First Line box. (Enter a value of .5" in the From Left box, for example, and a value of -.5" in the First Line box. You can use the arrows to the right for this step.)

To add bullets or numbers to existing paragraphs, don't bother with the Format Paragraph dialog box. Instead, select the paragraphs and then click the number or bullet button on the toolbar. Not only do you get your bullets and numbers, but also the paragraphs are correctly indented and formatted.

Paragraph spacing

1. To add space before a paragraph, increase the value in the Spacing Before box. To add space after, increase the value in the Spacing After box. The sample reflects your actions.

2. If you click on the arrows to the right, the values increment by .5, but you can be more precise, if you want. If you want a space before a title of 2.25 lines, for example, just type that value in the box. Although the sample doesn't show it, the setting works.

Most people just press Enter a bunch of times before and after a paragraph. If that works for you, don't bother with these steps.

Line spacing

Line spacing refers to the spacing of the lines within a paragraph. The default is single line spacing.

Six settings appear under Line Spacing, but for all practical purposes, you need to use only Auto, Single, 1.5 Lines, and Double. Use Auto if you have different-size fonts in the same paragraph, especially if they are very different in size. (How often does that come up?)

If you want more than double line spacing, increase the value under At. You can have line spacing of any size in Word for Windows. (If your boss likes a line spacing setting of 5.75, for example, you can do it.)

Paragraphs and pagination

If you want to format a paragraph to be always at the top of a page, such as a title, you can select the paragraph and, under Pagination, choose Page Break Before.

To be sure that no page breaks occur between two (or more) paragraphs, choose Keep With Next.

To be sure that a page break does not occur in the middle of a paragraph, choose Keep Lines Together.

Border Formatting

You can place a full border around your selection, or you can place a partial border around it. (I hear you — "What's a partial border?") Suppose that you want to put a line below a paragraph to set it off, but you don't want a full border. That's a partial border.

Adding a full border

1. Select the paragraph or object that you want to have a border.

2. Choose Border from the Format menu to open the Border Paragraphs dialog box (see the following figure).

3. Notice the three examples in the Preset box at the bottom left corner. Choose the second one (Box) if you don't want your border to have a shadow; choose the third one (Shadow) if you do.

4. Choose a border style from those available in the Line box on the right. Notice that each choice you make shows immediately in the Border sample area.

5. If you want the border to be farther away from the text it surrounds, increase the number in the From Text box under the sample. Just click on the up arrow to the right. Each click increases the distance by 1 point, which is reflected in the sample.

6. Click on OK.

Adding shading is different from adding a shadow. A shadow refers to the border itself. When the right and bottom lines of a border are thicker than the left and top lines, it produces a shadow effect. Shading, on the other hand, refers to adding shading within the selection. If you want the title row of a table to be shaded, for example, you don't choose Shadow; rather, you click the Shading button.

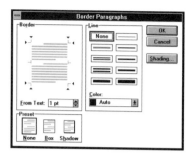

Here are two examples of borders around paragraphs:

This paragraph has an unshaded single border. This paragraph has an unshaded single border.

This paragraph has a shaded double border. This paragraph has a shaded double border.

Adding a partial border

1. Select the paragraph or object you want to have the partial border (or borders).

2. Open the Border Paragraphs dialog box. Notice the Border sample box in the upper left corner. Notice also the arrowheads: There are four in each corner of the sample. If you look closely, you see that they define each side of a paragraph. Two on top point at each other, two on the left and right sides point up and down, and two on the bottom point at each other; if you want to draw, for example, a straight line from one to another, you can).

3. Place the mouse pointer precisely between any two arrowheads that are pointing at each other and click once. Only those two arrowheads should show up.

4. Choose a line style. The sample should reflect your choice in the Border box.

5. To add a line to another side, just select that side; the line you selected for the first side then appears.

Removing a border

1. Select the paragraph or object that has the border you want to remove.
2. Open the Border Paragraphs dialog box. Click once on None in the Line box.

Making a border fit a paragraph

If you put a border around a sentence that does not extend from margin to margin, for example, the border still extends from margin to margin. You can easily correct this by changing the indentation of the border, which is another way of saying that you have to change the indentation of that paragraph. This process is explained in the section "Indentation," later in this part. (Do you see why this discussion is part of paragraph formatting?)

Adding shading

1. Select the paragraph or object you want to shade.
2. Open the Border Paragraphs dialog box. Click the Shading button on the right to open the Shading dialog box.
3. Notice the three choices in the Fill box under Custom: Pattern, Foreground, and Background. Click on the down arrow to the right of Pattern to open a pull-down menu of choices.
4. Choose 5% or 10%. These most commonly used fill percentages print better than do heavier ones. By all means, go ahead and experiment.
5. After you have selected the pattern of your choice, click on OK, which returns you to the Border Paragraph dialog box. The sample now shows the fill pattern you selected.

If you click on the down arrow next to Foreground or Background, you see a pull-down menu of color choices. Unless you have a color printer, these choices don't print, and, if you select a color just because it looks nice on-screen, you may be disappointed with the way it prints.

Don't be confused by "foreground" and "background." There really isn't any foreground or background, but you cannot have a pattern if you have only one color. That's why one has white selected and the other has black. The computer industry has settled on the terms "foreground" and "background" for the two colors needed to produce a variety of patterns. (Now you can impress your friends with this trivia.)

Frame Formatting

Frame formatting is complex and takes some practice.

1. If you want to try using frames, select a paragraph or another object and insert a frame from the Insert menu or from the toolbar.

2. Word for Windows prompts you to switch to Page Layout view if you are not already in that view. Click on OK.

3. When you are in Page Layout view, slowly move the mouse pointer into the framed object. Notice how the pointer changes to a four-headed arrow. When the pointer has this shape, you can click and drag on the framed object to move it anywhere on the page.

If you drop the object into text, the text wraps around it. You can also put a border around a framed object.

Picture Formatting

Picture formatting is similar to frame formatting in at least one respect: If you don't have a picture in your document, you cannot format one.

Picture formatting just means that you can select the picture and then either scale or crop it or both. When you *scale* a picture, you reduce or enlarge proportionally with no loss of picture; when you *crop* a picture, you reduce the size by cutting out some of the picture.

Tab Formatting

An important concept about tabs that even experienced typists seem to miss is that there are really two parts to any tab: the tab stop and the Tab key. You can set tab stops first or you can set them after you type the text — it doesn't matter.

Word for Windows has two types of tabs: the default tabs that appear on the ruler (see Part II) and customized tabs you can set yourself. You can use tab leaders with customized tabs.

Most people get along fine with the default tabs. When Word for Windows is installed, default tabs are set every half inch; every time you press Tab, the insertion point moves toward the right margin half an inch. The default tabs on the ruler are indicated by the small upside-down Ts.

To use the default tabs, just press Tab. To set customized tabs, choose Tabs from the Format menu to open the Tabs dialog box.

Changing the default tabs

Open the Tab dialog box. Change the value in the Default Tab Stops box and click the OK button. The ruler now shows the new default setting.

Changing the default tabs is quite unusual in one respect: It is the only tab action that affects the entire document rather than the selected paragraph. Fortunately, there isn't much reason to change the default tabs.

Setting customized tabs

Because customized tabs are paragraph specific, be sure that you have selected the paragraphs you want to have these tabs.

Most people use customized tabs to create columns of numbers. Although this method certainly works, let me suggest that you use the table feature instead. After you learn how tables work, you can see that they are a superior tool for this type of task.

If you insist on using tabs (go ahead — be that way), the easiest way to create your table is to just type the first line of the table and press Tab at the appropriate spots. Naturally, the table will not look right after you have entered that first line. Then set the customized tabs for the first line. Because you already have tabs in your text, the numbers line up with the tabs you place. Adjust as necessary. Then, every time you press Enter after typing a line, the tabs you set appear on the next line also.

This technique may take some practice, but you get the hang of it soon enough. You may even come to like it. (Yeah, right.)

The easiest way to set a customized tab is to choose the type of tab you want on the ribbon and then place the tab on the ruler. The four buttons with arrows on them on the right side of the ribbon are the tab buttons. You can use them to set (in order) left, center, right, and decimal tab stops.

Then move the mouse pointer to the ruler, below the vertical line that runs the length of the ruler. Click once where you want the tab, and the tab will appear on the ruler.

Setting tab leaders

To set tab leaders, you must use the Tab dialog box. A *tab leader* is a character that appears when you press the Tab key. Word for Windows offers four types of leaders: none, dot, dash, and underline.

In this example, a dot leader follows *Chapter One*.

I. Chapter One 5

Be sure that you select the paragraphs you want to have tab leaders and open the Tab dialog box.

Any existing customized tabs show up in the Tab Stop Position box. Either choose one or enter a number that corresponds to the place on the ruler where you want that tab to appear.

If necessary, define the alignment of the tab. Next, choose the type of leader you want.

When you have made all your choices, click the Set button and then click on OK. The tabs you set appear on the ruler. There is no indication of the tab leader. You must press Tab to see the leader appear in your document.

Removing tabs

The topic of removing tabs refers, naturally, to removing any custom tabs. There isn't any reason to try to remove the default tabs.

Custom tabs appear as small arrows in the ruler. All you have to do to remove one is to click and drag it down off the ruler.

You can clear all the custom tabs on the ruler at one time by using the Tab dialog box and clicking on the Clear All button.

TIP When you remove custom tabs, you remove them from only selected paragraphs. To remove them from the entire document, first select the entire document (choose Select All from the Edit menu) and then open the Tab dialog box and click the Clear All button. Notice that, when you select the entire document, even if you have custom tabs, no tabs show on the ruler or in the dialog box. That's just a bug — you still remove the tabs by following the preceding procedure.

Document and Section Formatting

Document formatting and section formatting in Word for Windows are closely related. The reason is that some procedures and settings apply to the entire document. If you want one part of the document to have a different setting from another, you must create sections. You can format a section of a document as though you were formatting the entire document. Another way of saying this is that, if there were no sections in Word for Windows, you would have to create a separate document every time you wanted to change one of these settings. So, you learn to live with sections.

Every Word for Windows document has at least one section and can have as many as you deem necessary. When you insert a section break, it is displayed as a double dotted line across the screen. You can tell which section you are in by looking at the status bar at the bottom of the screen. (It's kind of like touring in a strange city: You can find out which section you're in by checking a bar.)

Inserting a section break

1. Place the insertion point where you want the section break to occur.
2. Choose Break from the Insert menu to open the Break dialog box.
3. Select the type of section break you want to insert. (The type of section break you need depends on what you're doing. See the individual instructions in the remainder of this section to determine the type of section break for each of them.)

Adding a header or footer to a document

A *header* is text or a graphic that appears at the top of every page in the margin. A *footer* is text or a graphic that appears at the bottom of every page in the margin. Other than that, there isn't any difference between the two.

1. Choose Header/Footer from the View menu to open the Header/Footer dialog box.
2. Choose Header. (To show some independence, choose Footer instead.)
3. Press the OK button. The header/footer pane appears on-screen (see the following figure).
4. Enter the header.
5. Format the header as you want, by using normal editing procedures.
6. Click once on the OK button. Now you have a header on every page of your document. (Footers work in the same way.)

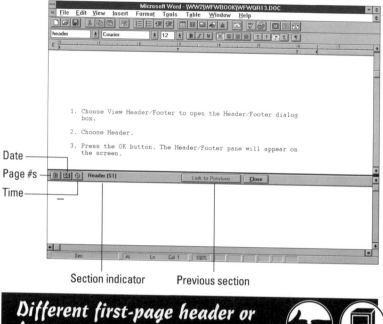

Date

Page #s

Time

Section indicator   Previous section

Different first-page header or footer

1. To get a different first-page header or footer, open the Header/
   Footer dialog box.
2. Put a check in the Different First Page option. (**Note:** At this
   point, if your dialog box does not show the four header and
   footer options just illustrated, you are in page layout view.
   You're better off stopping now and changing to normal view.)

Word for Windows has a header and footer feature called
Different First Page. You can use this feature to suppress a header
or footer on the first page, or you can enter a different header or
footer on the first page. Here we have the beginning of confusion.
A header or footer that is different on the first page is not, according
to Word for Windows, a different header or footer. Got that?

Word for Windows considers a different header or footer as one
you want to change somewhere inside the document (the header
Chapter One, for example, from the earlier example, becomes
Chapter Two). Simple, isn't it?

You can get several different combinations by using this option,
as follows.

**Same header and footer throughout the document or section,
but no header (or footer) on the first page**

What a mouthful. All this means is that you can, for example, add page numbers (footers) to your document on every page, *including* the first page, and add a header to every page *except* the first page.

1. You have to use the View Header/Footer dialog box three separate times for this procedure (*three times!*).
2. Create the header.
3. Create the first header.
4. Create the footer (not the first footer). Seems tedious (and it is), but it works.

No (or different) header or footer on the first page

1. Open the Header/Footer dialog box.
2. Put a check in the Different First Page box if one isn't already there.
3. Choose Header (or Footer, if that's what you want) and click on OK. The header/footer pane appears. Enter your header (or footer), format it, and close the pane.

   If you don't want a header (or footer) on the first page, stop here. If you want to create a different header (or footer) on the first page, go to step 4.
4. Repeat steps 1 and 2. Then choose First Header (or First Footer) and click on OK. Now you can create your first page header (or footer).

Different header and footer on the first page of the section

1. For this procedure, you must use the Header/Footer dialog box four times (yep — four times).
2. Create the regular header.
3. Create the regular footer.
4. Create the first header.
5. Create the first footer.

What a palaver! This is the penalty you pay, though, for using different headers and footers on the first page of your document.

Different odd and even pages

You can use this option if you want a different header or footer for odd and even pages, such as aligning the page numbers on the right on odd pages, and on the left on even pages.

Keep in mind that this option is unusual in one major respect: If you select it, it applies to the entire document regardless of the number of sections in the document.

Changing the header or footer in a document

1. To change a header or footer within a document, you first must insert a section break.
2. Press F5 (GoTo), type the page number where you want to begin the new header or footer, and press Enter.
3. Insert a section break from the Insert Break menu and choose Next Page under Section Break. The section break appears on your screen.
4. You can now enter the new header or footer as described. The first-page options apply here, too, as they do for each section.

Editing an existing header or footer

1. If you want to edit an existing header, be sure that the insertion point is in the correct section for that header (or footer).
2. Open the Header/Footer dialog box.
3. Choose the appropriate selection (header or footer) and click on the OK button. This step opens the Header/Footer pane, which displays the existing header or footer.
4. Modify the header or footer as you would do with any text.
5. Click on OK to close the pane.

Using the Link to Previous button in the Header/Footer pane

The Link to Previous button is used only when you have more than one header or footer in your document. This button means, by definition, that you also have more than one section in your document. If you want one section in your document to have the same header or footer as the previous section, you can use this option.

Choosing this button copies the header or footer from the previous section to the current section. The previous header or footer is also copied to all sections that have the same header or footer as does the current section.

Column Formatting (Newspaper Style)

Column formatting does not refer to columns in a table (see Part V). Instead, this phrase refers to what some people call *snaking columns*. You can format the entire document for snaking columns or you can format a part of it.

Formatting an entire document with snaking columns

1. Choose Columns from the Format menu to open the Columns dialog box.
2. Select the number of columns you want and whether you want them separated by a vertical line. You can also adjust the spacing between columns.
3. Click on OK.

Formatting part of the document with snaking columns

1. Select the text you want to be in columns.
2. Open the Columns dialog box.
3. Select the number of columns you want and whether you want them separated by a vertical line. You can also adjust the spacing between columns.
4. In the Apply To box, choose Selected Text (which, by the way, does not show up as an option unless you select text first). This step tells Word for Windows to insert the proper section breaks.
5. Click on OK.

The easiest way to format with snaking columns is to create the document and then come back and select the text you want to be in columns. That way, Word for Windows handles the section breaks for you. Otherwise, you must put them in yourself. (Why bother?)

Footnote Formatting

Footnotes are references that have two parts: the footnote reference mark in the text itself and the footnote, which usually appears at the bottom of the page. With Word for Windows, you can choose to have footnotes appear directly below the text, at the end of a section, or at the end of the document.

You delete a footnote in Word for Windows by deleting the reference mark in the text, not by deleting the footnote itself. If you try to delete the footnote itself, you get an error message. When you delete the reference mark in the text, the entire footnote disappears. If you are using numbered footnotes, the remaining footnotes automatically adjust their numbering for you. (Now *there's* a nice feature.) Unfortunately, the same is not true of footnotes that use letters. (Now, *there's* a terrible feature.)

Inserting a numbered footnote

1. To insert a footnote, be sure that the insertion point is at the appropriate spot in the text and then choose Foot<u>n</u>ote from the <u>I</u>nsert menu.
2. Click on OK. This step opens the footnote pane, where you then can enter your footnote text. (The footnote pane is a cousin of the Header/Footer pane.) After you have entered the text, click once on the Close button.
3. To continue entering footnotes, place the insertion point at the appropriate places in the text and repeat steps 1 and 2. The numbers automatically increment by one.
4. If you insert a footnote between two existing footnotes, the numbers automatically adjust in the text and in the footnotes themselves. This is also true when you delete a numbered footnote.

Using letters or symbols in footnotes

1. Open the Footnote dialog box.
2. In the <u>C</u>ustom Footnote Mark box, type the letter or symbol you want to use.
3. Click on OK.

Deleting a footnote

1. Select the footnote reference mark in the text.
2. Delete the reference mark. Now the footnote is gone.

 You might find it difficult to find a footnote in your document, especially if you haven't used that document for some time. Fortunately, Word for Windows provides an easy method. Press F5 (which displays the words GoTo in the status bar at the bottom of the screen). Then type **F** followed by the number of the footnote. (Even if you used letters or symbols, you must type the number of the footnote — if it is the third footnote in the document, you have to type 3.) Word for Windows brings you directly to that footnote.

Viewing a footnote

Simply choose Footnotes from the View menu. (If the Footnotes option isn't available, there are no footnotes in the document, no matter what you think.)

Using footnote options

Footnote placement

To change the placement of footnotes for the entire document, just follow the steps in this section. If you want to change them for just a part of the document, you first must insert a section break. This type of section break can be continuous, especially if you want to change the placement more than once on the same page. Just make sure that you position the insertion point at the location where you want to change the footnote position.

1. Open the Footnotes dialog box and choose Options to open the Footnote Options dialog box.
2. Click on the down arrow to the right of the Place At box. This step shows you the choices you have.
3. Select the option you want and click on OK.

Footnote numbering

1. Open the Footnotes dialog box and choose Options to open the Footnote Options dialog box.

2. Either enter the number you want your footnotes to begin with or use the arrows to the right of the Start At box.

3. If you want the footnote numbers to begin at 1 in each new section of your document, be sure that there is an X in the Restart Each Section box.

4. Click on OK.

To change the footnote numbering sequence within a document, you have to insert a section break every time you want to change the numbering sequence. You can begin the numbering sequence at any number you want for each section in the document.

Footnote separators

A footnote separator is the line that separates a footnote from the text on a page and the line that separates a footnote continued from a previous page. It also refers to the continuation notice you might want to enter to alert readers that the footnote is continued. You can change any of these options by choosing the appropriate button from the Footnote dialog box.

Margin, Page-Size, and Paper-Feed Formatting

A *margin* is the white space between the edge of the page and the spot where your text begins. When Word for Windows is first installed, it sets the default margins to 1 inch for the top and bottom and 1.25 inches for the left and right margins. You can change these defaults whenever you want either for a single document, or you can change the default so that every new document starts with your new margins.

You can also change the paper size and orientation, for either your entire document or just part of it. And, as with margins, you can change the default settings so that all new documents use a different orientation or page size than the original default.

Finally, Word for Windows provides several paper-feed options for you to use if you have a printer that takes advantage of them.

Word for Windows does all this from the Page Setup dialog box, which is in three parts. Actually, it's like three different dialog boxes, but rather than open each one from the menu, you use the dialog box (see the next figure.)

Let's see how this stuff works.

Page Setup
Select which page attributes to modify.
⦿ <u>M</u>argins ○ <u>S</u>ize and Orientation ○ <u>P</u>aper Source

		Sample
<u>T</u>op:	1"	
<u>B</u>ottom:	1"	
<u>L</u>eft:	1"	
<u>R</u>ight:	1"	
<u>G</u>utter:	0"	

☐ <u>F</u>acing Pages   <u>A</u>pply To: Whole Document

| OK | Cancel | <u>U</u>se as Default... |

Setting margins for a document

1. Choose Page Set<u>u</u>p from the Forma<u>t</u> menu to open the Page Setup dialog box.
2. Make changes to the settings, by either typing the new values directly in the boxes or using the arrows to the right of the settings boxes. Note that the sample reflects your new settings (but only if you use the arrows to change the settings).
3. Click on OK. Your margins are now in effect.

Setting margins for portions of a document

1. Make sure that the insertion point is on the first page in which you want to make the margin change.
2. Open the Page Setup dialog box.
3. Make the margin changes you want.
4. Click on the down arrow to the right of the <u>A</u>pply To box in the bottom right corner and choose This Point Forward. Now your document has the new margins from the current page to the end of the document.
5. To change the margins back to the original settings later in the document, place the insertion point somewhere on the first subsequent page that gets the original margins.
6. Repeat steps 3 and 4. Now your document has three sets of margins.

When you change margins for a portion of your document as described in these steps, you are also creating sections at the same time. If you follow these instructions and go to the last page of your document, you see that you are in section three. The fact that Word for Windows creates the sections for you relieves you of having to worry about it. (Unless you like worrying about such things.)

Changing the default margins

1. Follow the steps outlined earlier, in the section "Setting margins for a document."

2. When you have made your changes, click the <u>U</u>se as Default button in the lower right corner of the dialog box. A confirmation message asks you whether you really want to do this (as though you would go to all this trouble if you didn't). Just click on OK. All new documents based on that template have the new margins.

Changing the size and orientation of the page

You can change not only your margins but also the orientation (portrait versus landscape) and the size of the page, for either the entire document or selected sections.

Changing the size and orientation for the entire document

1. Open the Page Setup dialog box.
2. At the top of the dialog box, choose <u>S</u>ize and Orientation.
3. Make the changes you want. Notice that the sample reflects your changes.
4. Click on OK when you finish.

Changing the size and orientation for part of the document

1. Make sure that the insertion point is on the first page on which you want to make the change.
2. Open the Page Setup dialog box and switch to <u>S</u>ize and Orientation.

3. Make the changes you want.

4. Click on the down arrow to the right of the <u>A</u>pply To box in the bottom right corner and choose This Point Forward. Now your document has the new margins from the current page to the end of the document.

5. To change the page size or orientation back to the original settings later in the document, place the insertion point somewhere on the first subsequent page that gets the original size and orientation.

6. Repeat steps 3 and 4.

Changing the default size and orientation

1. Follow the steps outlined earlier, in the section "Changing the size and orientation for the entire document."

2. When you have made your changes, click the <u>U</u>se as Default button in the lower right corner of the dialog box. Just click on OK when the confirmation message appears.

Using paper-feed options

This option enables you to select different paper feeds, depending on your printer. If you have a laser printer, just be sure that Default Tray is selected for <u>F</u>irst Page and <u>O</u>ther Pages. If you have a multiple-feed printer, you can easily configure the feed options to suit yourself.

Page Numbering

Page numbering can be simple (number every page from 1 to the end of the document) or complex (no page number on the first page or restart page numbering from 1 in the middle of the document, for example).

If you put page numbers at the top of the page, they are headers. If you put them at the bottom of the page they are footers.

When you enter a page number in the manner described in the following section, you enter a field code. A *field code* is a device that does all the work for you, so if you add or delete pages in your document, the page numbering takes care of itself.

If you want to see the code rather than the page number, choose Field Codes from the View menu. Be sure to turn it off again or you run the risk of confusing yourself later.

The simplest way to add page numbers to your document is to choose Page Numbers from the Insert menu and make the appropriate choices from the Page Numbers dialog box. This method, however, doesn't give you any flexibility with your page numbers (such as adding the word *page* in front of the number). If you need more flexibility with your page numbers, follow the steps in this section.

Adding page numbers to every page in the document

1. Open the Header/Footer dialog box.
2. Choose Footer (or Header, if appropriate). Then click on OK.
3. Notice the three icons to the left of the pane. Click once on the first one, the Page button. This action adds page numbers. Simple, isn't it?
4. Format as you want (center or bold, for example). If you want to add the word *page* or put a dash before and after the page number, you can do it here.
5. Click on OK.

Adding page numbering except for the first page

1. Open the Header/Footer dialog box.
2. Choose Different First Page and then choose Footer (*not* First Footer).
3. Click once on the OK button.
4. Choose the page button in the Header/Footer pane, format the way you want, and click on Close.

Starting page numbering at 1 after the first page

This is a tricky little procedure. Follow the steps closely or you might not get the results you want.

1. If you have already entered page numbers for the document or section, delete them first.
2. Go to the top of the second page of the document or section.
3. Choose Break from the Insert menu, choose Next Page under Section Break, and click on OK. This step causes a section break (two lines running across the screen) to appear on-screen.
4. Be sure that your insertion point is in the new section.
5. Open the Header/Footer dialog box. If Different First Page is on, turn it off.
6. Choose Footer or Header and then click once on the Page Numbers button on the right side of the dialog box. This step opens the Page Number Format dialog box.
7. Choose your number Format, and click on OK.
8. Click on OK in the Header/Footer dialog box to open the Header/Footer pane.
9. Click the page button in the Header/Footer pane, format the way you want, and click on Close.

Changing the starting page number (higher than 1)

1. Open the Header/Footer dialog box and choose a footer (or header, if appropriate).
2. Click once on the Page Numbers button to the right of the dialog box to open the Page Number Format dialog box. In the Start At box, type whatever number you want to start your paging.
3. Click on OK twice to open the Header/Footer pane.
4. Click the page button in the Header/Footer pane, format the way you want, and click on Close.

Selecting different styles for page numbers

1. Open the Header/Footer dialog box and choose either Header or Footer.
2. Open the Page Number Format dialog box by clicking the Page Numbers button.
3. Click on the down arrow to the right of the numbers in the Number Format field. This step shows the different styles of numbers available to you. Choose the style you want by clicking once on it.

Pagination

Word for Windows automatically paginates your document as you type it, depending on a number of variables: the size and orientation of your page, font and size, line spacing, indentation settings, and whether orphan and widow control is turned on. The type of page break Word for Windows inserts is called a soft page break. A *soft page break* fluctuates depending on your editing actions. If you delete text from a page, for example, text from the next page moves up to the current page. A soft page break is represented by a thin dotted line running across the screen.

Soft page breaks sometimes do not adjust immediately. This can be confusing when you have added or deleted text and you're sure that the page break should have moved. If you wait just a few seconds, you see the dotted line move to the correct spot.

A *hard page break* is a page break you insert manually. Hard page breaks do not fluctuate because Word for Windows assumes that you want that page break right where you put it. Therefore, to eliminate a hard page break, you must delete it. A hard page break is represented by a single solid line running across the page.

Inserting a hard page break

1. Place the insertion point where you want the page break to appear.
2. Press Ctrl+Enter.

Deleting a hard page break

1. Place the insertion point just below the page break and press Backspace.
2. Or place the insertion point on the hard page break and press Del.

Formatting a Section Layout (Vertical Alignment and Line Numbering)

You can format a section for vertical alignment and to include line numbering. You might use vertical alignment for a title page, for example. Make the title page a section and vertically align the title to be centered.

Line numbers are rarely used by anyone outside of law firms. If you have to use them, you can format any section (or sections) in your document to include line numbers. (You can see line numbers only in print preview and when you print the document.)

Style Formatting (An Automated Approach)

A style (in computer terminology) is simply an automated way of applying formatting to your documents. A *style* is a group of formats you name and save. Styles in Word for Windows are paragraph related, which means that you apply styles to paragraphs rather than to individual characters.

When you use styles, rather than apply formatting directly to the paragraph, you assign a code name to your formatting. This code name is called a style. Then you apply the style to selected paragraphs. Later, if you want to change the formatting in those paragraphs, rather than change the paragraphs directly, you simply change the style definition, and the changes occur dynamically throughout your document in each paragraph that has that style assigned to it. Good stuff, eh?

Word for Windows saves your styles with the documents in which you create them. Because you can copy styles between documents and templates, you have to create a set of styles only one time.

Word for Windows comes with a default set of styles you can redefine but not delete. So, don't be surprised if you want to delete, for example, the Heading 2 style and Word for Windows doesn't let you. You also cannot rename these styles.

Direct formatting always takes precedence over styles. That is, you can format a paragraph directly regardless of whether it has a style applied to it.

Many facets to styles cannot be covered in this book. The instructions that follow guide you through the most common uses of styles.

With a little practice, you should be able to become proficient in the use of styles fairly quickly. You will find that styles are easy to use and are terrifically efficient.

Creating Styles

By using styles, you can apply a set of formats at one time rather than one by one. You can use a number of methods to create a style. The best thing to do is pick a method and stick with it until you know more about styles. Let me suggest that you follow the steps in the section "Creating a style by example" (in which you format a paragraph the way you want and then use that paragraph to create the new style). That method is by far the easiest.

Creating styles by using the Format Style Menu

1. Choose Style from the Format menu to open the Style dialog box (see the following figure.)

2. In the Style Name box, type a name for the style. It's best to keep the name short and simple, but try to be a little descriptive.

3. If you want, assign a shortcut keystroke to the style. You can use this keystroke to apply the style.

4. Click the Define button to see the full dialog box. Don't panic — it looks worse than it is. The buttons just take you to the different dialog boxes in which you can choose formats for your style.

5. Under Change Formatting, choose the various buttons to specify formats for the style. Choose the Character button, for example, to specify a different font for the style.

6. When the Description box shows all the formats you want for the style, choose the Add to Template button to create the style.

7. To create more styles, repeat steps 2 through 6 for each new style.

8. When you finish creating your styles, click the Apply button.

Creating a style by example

1. Select the paragraph with the formats you want for the style.
2. Double-click in the style box (the first box in the ribbon).
3. Type a name for the style.
4. To create the style, click outside the style box. That's it. (Now, admit it. Wasn't that easier than going through all that menu stuff?)

Applying a style by using the Format Style menu

1. Select the paragraph or paragraphs you want to have the style.
2. From the Format menu, choose Style to open the Style dialog box.
3. In the Style Name box, select the style you want to apply.
4. Click the Apply button.
5. Click on Close.

Applying a style with the ribbon

This method is the easiest way to apply styles.

1. Select the paragraph or paragraphs you want to have the style.
2. Click on the down arrow to the right of the style box on the ribbon to see the available styles. (You may have to scroll to see all the styles.)
3. Click on the style you want. It is applied immediately to the selected paragraph (or paragraphs).

Applying a style with a shortcut key

1. Select the paragraph you want to have the style.
2. Press the keystroke. (Don't forget to use any combination keys that are part of the shortcut.)

Don't forget — you cannot use a shortcut key if you didn't assign one in the first place. If you are sick and tired of using that ribbon and you desperately want to use your trusty old keyboard, you can create a shortcut keystroke for a style whenever you want: Open the Style dialog box, select the style, and assign the shortcut keystroke.

Changing a style by using the Format Style menu

1. From the Format menu, choose Style to open the Style dialog box.
2. In the Style Name box, select the name of the style you want to change.
3. Click the Define button.
4. Under Change Formatting, choose the appropriate buttons to change formats for the style. You can choose the Character button, for example, to change the character formatting.
5. When the Description box shows all the formats you want for the style, choose the Change button to change the style.
6. Click on Apply and then on Close. Now all the paragraphs formatted with that style have the new formats.

Changing a style by using the ribbon

Again, this is the easiest way to change a style.

1. Select a paragraph formatted with the style you want to change.
2. Make the formatting changes you want.
3. With the insertion point in the reformatted paragraph, click the style box in the ribbon.
4. Click in the document window.
5. When Word for Windows displays a message asking whether you want to redefine the style, choose the Yes button.

TIP You can use this method to quickly reapply a style when you have formatted a paragraph you didn't mean to format (assuming that the paragraph in question was formatted by using styles). Follow steps 1 through 4 and, when Word for Windows asks whether you want to redefine the style, click on No. The original style formats are reapplied to the paragraph.

Deleting a style

You can delete styles you no longer need.

1. Choose Style from the Format menu to open the Style dialog box.

2. Type or select the name of the style you want to delete.

3. Click the Define button.

4. Choose the Delete button. Word for Windows displays a message asking you to confirm the deletion.

5. To delete the style, click the Yes button.

6. Choose the Close button.

When you delete a style, any paragraphs in the document that are formatted with that style revert to the Normal style. Also, you cannot delete a standard style that comes with Word for Windows.

Merging styles between documents and templates

1. Choose Style from the Format menu to open the Style dialog box.

2. Click the Define button.

3. Click the Merge button to open the Merge Styles dialog box.

4. First select the document or template in the File Name box and then choose the From Template button. When the message appears asking whether you want to replace styles with the same name, choose the Yes button to update styles. If you say No, nothing happens.

5. To close the Style dialog box, choose the Close button.

To use styles in a current document that you created in a previous document, you can copy the styles from that document to your current one. You cannot copy individual styles; you get the whole set.

If you decide to merge styles from another document or template into your current document, any incoming styles that have the same name as styles in your current document overwrite them. This isn't a problem if both styles have the same definition; if your current document has styles with the same name but a different definition, however, you have a problem.

Viewing styles

You can see the styles that are applied to each paragraph. This beats guessing at them or clicking in the paragraph to see what the ribbon says.

1. Choose Options from the Tools menu to open the Options dialog box.

2. If the View category in the Category list on the left isn't already selected, go ahead and select it. You may have to scroll to the top of the category list to see it.

3. In the Window box on the right, where it says Style Area Width, enter a value of .5 (or use the up arrow to the right).

4. Click on OK. Your screen now shows a vertical line on the left where you can see the style names you use.

5. You can close the style area in the same manner. Or, you can use the mouse. Place the mouse pointer carefully on the vertical line until the pointer changes shape. When it does, you can click and drag to move the line.

Printing style descriptions

You can print descriptions of the styles in your document to use as a reference.

1. Choose Print from the File menu to open the Print dialog box.

2. Click on the down arrow to the right of the Print box. It should say Document.

3. Choose Styles.

4. Click on OK. The styles in the document will now print.

Part V
Word for Windows Tables

Tables are, arguably, the single best feature in Word for Windows.

Perhaps the main use of tables in Word for Windows is to construct financial rows and columns. Tables can also be used, however, to arrange paragraphs side by side so that you don't have to press Enter at the end of each line and press Tab to move to each paragraph. (Many people still use this early approach to side-by-side paragraphs. There's nothing wrong with it until it comes time to modify the text — then it's either time to go home sick or call a temp.)

Tables are constructed of rows (they run across the screen) and columns (they run up and down the screen). The box in which a row and column meet is called a *cell*. So much for the terminology.

You can put anything in a cell except for another table. When you type in a cell, the text wraps within the cell (which is the way side-by-side paragraphs work).

When you first insert a table, regardless of the number of columns (you can have as many as 31), Word for Windows inserts the table from margin to margin, with each column having the same size. You can modify these settings after the table has been inserted.

You can add and delete rows, columns, and individual cells, and you can resize rows, columns, and cells individually. You can use decimal tabs within a table to align financial data.

To get the full power of Word for Windows, start using tables. As an example, all the tables in this book were created by using the Word for Windows table feature.

Creating Tables

Almost everything you can do with a table can be found under the Table menu. The only exceptions are that you format text by using the normal formatting procedures and that you can add things such as footnotes by using the normal footnote procedures.

1. Choose Insert Table from the Table menu to open the Insert Table dialog box.

2. Enter the Number of Columns and Number of Rows you want.

3. Click on OK. The table gridlines should be displayed on-screen. If they are not, choose Gridlines from the Table menu. If they still don't show up, you didn't insert the table correctly. Try again.

You can use the toolbar to insert a table. Click once on the 12th button from the left to display a grid underneath the button. Place the mouse pointer in the first box in the grid and then click and drag. The grid shows you how many rows and columns you have selected. This technique may take a little practice, but it's harmless, so go ahead and try. If you insert an incorrectly sized table, just press Undo and try again.

Editing Tables

When you *edit* a table, you alter its structure in some way. The following steps show you procedures for editing your Word for Windows tables.

For more information, see Chapter 12 of *Word for Windows For Dummies*.

Inserting columns

1. Be sure that your insertion point is somewhere in the column.

2. Choose Insert Cells from the Table menu to open the Insert Cells dialog box.

3. Choose Insert Entire Column.

4. Click on OK.

When you insert or delete a column, the overall size of the table changes. If you insert a column in a table that already occupied the space from margin to margin, you have to adjust the overall width of the table. This procedure is explained later in this part.

TIP

You can quickly select one or more columns with the mouse by placing the mouse pointer in the first column to be selected and clicking the *right* mouse button. This technique selects the entire column. If you click and drag using the right mouse button, you can select multiple columns. If you select multiple columns and then select Insert Columns from the Ta̲ble menu (no dialog box appears if you use this shortcut), Word for Windows inserts an equal number of blank columns.

Inserting rows

1. Be sure that your insertion point is somewhere in the row.

2. Choose I̲nsert Cells from the Ta̲ble menu to open the Insert Cells dialog box.

3. Choose Insert Entire R̲ow.

4. Click on OK.

TIP

You can quickly select a row in a table by placing the mouse pointer directly to the left of the row outside the table so that the pointer is an arrow pointing toward the upper right. Clicking once selects the entire row; clicking and dragging selects multiple rows. If you select the entire row, no dialog box appears when you insert something. If you select multiple rows, an equal number of blank rows is inserted just above the ones you selected.

Inserting cells

1. Be sure that your insertion point is in the cell just to the right of (or above) where you want the new cell to appear.

2. Choose Insert Cells from the Ta̲ble menu to open the Insert Cells dialog box.

3. Choose whether you want adjacent cells shifted down or to the right.

4. Click on OK.

This procedure throws your table out of alignment because the column or row (depending on your choice in step 3) where you add the new cell expands, but other columns and rows don't expand. Other than specialized situations, there isn't much reason to use this feature.

Deleting columns

1. Be sure that your insertion point is somewhere in the column.

2. Choose <u>D</u>elete Cells from the T<u>a</u>ble menu to open the Delete Cells dialog box.

3. Choose Delete Entire <u>C</u>olumn.

4. Click on OK.

5. Refer to the Tip in the section "Inserting columns," at the beginning of this part.

Be careful with this procedure. If you delete the wrong column or delete a column when you meant to insert it and you don't catch the error right away, you may have quite a bit of work to do to re-create the lost column. (The Lost Column — sounds like a bad movie.)

Deleting rows

1. Be sure that your insertion point is somewhere in the row.

2. Choose <u>D</u>elete Cells from the T<u>a</u>ble menu to open the Delete Cells dialog box.

3. Choose Insert Entire <u>R</u>ow.

4. Click on OK.

5. Refer to the Tip in the section "Inserting rows" in this part. Also, look at the Remember note in the section "Deleting columns."

Deleting cells

1. Be sure that your insertion point is in the cell you want to delete. Or, click in the first cell to be deleted and drag to include all the cells you want to delete. If the cells you want to delete aren't connected, you have to perform this operation more than once. (What? Yup — even Word for Windows has its limitations.)

2. Choose <u>D</u>elete Cells from the T<u>a</u>ble menu to open the Delete Cells dialog box.

3. Select whether you want adjacent cells shifted up or to the left.

4. Click on OK.

5. Refer to the Remember note in the section "Inserting cells."

Changing the column width

1. Be sure that the insertion point is somewhere in the column.

2. Choose Select Column from the Table menu to select the entire column.

3. Choose Column Width from the Table menu to open the Column Width dialog box (see the following figure). You can then enter a value or use the arrows to the right to change the value.

4. To change the width of other columns, click either the Previous Column or Next Column button and enter values for them.

5. When you have finished, click on OK.

Column Width	
Width of Column 3:	1.69"	OK
Space between Cols:	0.15"	Cancel
Previous Column	Next Column

TIP — Don't forget to select the column (see step 2 in the preceding list). Otherwise, you change the width of only the cell in which the insertion point is located. Of course, if you want to change only the width of a cell or group of cells, you have to select only the cell (or cells) involved. If you do this, however, your table will no longer be symmetrically aligned.

TIP — You can use the mouse to change the column width, but it takes some practice. You place the tip of the mouse arrow precisely on the right vertical gridline of the column you want to resize and then just click and drag. Be sure to wait until the pointer changes shape. This technique changes the size of the table as well as the column because the other columns don't adjust automatically.

If you don't want the overall size of the table to change, press Ctrl before you click and drag. This step, however, also changes the size of columns to the right of the one you're dragging. (Something has to give if you're resizing a column but you don't want the overall width of the table to change.) If you have changed their size previously, you may be upset to see that Word for Windows changes them again. This procedure is another one you would be wise to practice before trying it in a critical situation.

Changing the row height

1. Be sure that the insertion point is somewhere in the row.

2. Choose Select Row from the Table menu to select the entire row.

3. Choose Row Height from the Table menu to open the Row Height dialog box. You can then enter a value in the At box.

4. If you want to change the height of other rows, click the Previous Column or Next Column buttons.

5. When you have finished, click on OK.

Row height is set by default to Automatic and expands automatically (see why they call it Automatic?) as the text you add wraps. Unless you're designing a form (a process that is not discussed in this book), there probably isn't any reason to change this setting. You may need to use other elements in the Row Height dialog box, however, for other reasons. These elements are covered elsewhere in this part. The following figure shows the Row Height dialog box.

Moving rows and columns

1. Be sure that the insertion point is in the column or row to be moved.

2. Choose either Select Row or Select Column from the Table menu to select the column or row you want to move.

3. Choose Cut from the Edit menu. The column or row disappears from the table.

4. Place the insertion point as follows: For a row, place it in the row underneath where you want to insert the row you cut; for a column, place it in the column to the right of where you want to insert the cut column. Don't worry — if you get it wrong, you can always press Undo and try again. (Also, see the second Tip in this section for more information about this operation.)

5. Choose Paste Rows (or Paste Columns, if you cut a column) from the Edit menu. The row or column should appear in the correct spot.

6. Repeat as necessary.

You probably will have to switch the position of columns and rows at some point when you use tables. Fortunately, this procedure is easy in Word for Windows. It is a little tricky, though, to move a column or row to become the last column or row in the table (see the second Tip in this section for instructions).

If you feel adventurous, you may want to try a shortcut method with the mouse. This technique is very quick and easy to use, but it's also easy to make mistakes. Try it, and you be the judge. Select either the row or column you want to move. Then, instead of cutting, move the mouse pointer into the selection until the pointer becomes an arrow that points toward the upper left. You are now in *drag-and-drop* mode. (**Note:** If your pointer doesn't change shape, the drag-and-drop feature may be turned off. To check the setting, choose Options from the Tools menu to open the Options dialog box. Under Category on the left, select General. The third setting is Drag-and-drop. An X in the box to the left means that it is turned on.) After the pointer is in the correct shape, just click and drag to the new location. The column or row should appear in the new spot.

This tip applies to situations in which you want to move a column or row to become the last column or row in the table. In these instances, first be sure that your nonprinting characters are showing on-screen. You do this by clicking once on the Show All button, which is the last button on the ribbon (the one that looks like a paragraph mark). When this button is on, you should be able to see paragraph marks, tabs, spaces between words, and so on, on your screen.

Let's begin by describing the column procedure. Notice that each cell in the table contains a funny-looking symbol, which is always located directly after the contents of the cell. This *end-of-cell marker* acts just like a paragraph symbol in normal text. Notice also that a set of these symbols is just to the right of the last column in the table. To move a column to the end of the table, you have to select these symbols. In fact, that's why they're there. You can select them with the mouse by precisely placing the mouse pointer on one of them and clicking the right mouse button. You can select them with the keyboard by placing the insertion point in a cell just to the left, pressing the right-arrow key (not the Tab key), and then choosing Select Column from the Table menu. Got all that?

To move a row to the end of the table, select the first paragraph mark beneath the table.

Aligning a table between the left and right margins

1. Select the entire table by placing the insertion point somewhere in the table and choosing Select Table from the Table menu.

2. Choose Row Height from the Table menu to open the Row Height menu. (That's right — Row Height. Hard to believe, isn't it?)

3. To indent the table a specific distance, enter a value in the Indent from Left box. Or, you can center or right-align the table by making your choice in the Alignment box.

This procedure applies only if the table doesn't currently occupy the entire space between the left and right margins. Also, the process of aligning tables does not affect the text in cells. To format the text in cells, just use normal formatting procedures.

If you don't select the entire table first, only the row where the insertion point is located is affected. The table, of course, is thrown out of alignment.

Merging cells

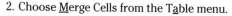

1. Select the cells you want to merge.

2. Choose Merge Cells from the Table menu.

The process of merging cells is useful when you want, for example, to center a heading over several columns. As usual, you should keep some things in mind. You cannot merge nonconnected cells. You cannot merge a cell that has been merged previously. (If you want to merge several cells, for example, and Merge Cells isn't available from the Table menu, one or more of the selected cells was previously merged. You first have to split that merged cell and then you can merge all the cells at one time.) Splitting cells is the way you reverse the merge cell operation.

TIP When you merge cells, Word for Windows inserts a paragraph mark in the resulting merged cell for each cell that was merged except for the resulting merged cell. What the heck does *that* mean? If you merge five cells, for example, the resulting single merged cell contains four paragraph marks, or *returns*. The effect is that the row containing the merged cells expands to accommodate all those returns. So, before you continue, you should delete all those returns (unless you have some reason to keep them).

Splitting cells

1. Select the cell that has been merged.

2. Choose Split Cells from the Table menu.

The Split Cells option does not show on the Table menu unless the insertion point is in a merged cell.

Splitting a table into two or more tables

1. Place the insertion point somewhere in the row just below where the split will occur. It's not necessary to have the insertion point in the first cell.

2. Press Ctrl+Shift and then press Enter.

You may find this feature useful for several reasons. Sometimes, for example, you have to build what appears to be several tables but that are really all the same in terms of structure and formatting. The only reason that there are several tables is that text is between them. You can build them all as one table, accomplish all your formatting in one operation, and then split the table and insert the text between the split elements of the table.

If the table is the first item in your document and you want to insert a return above the table, just be sure that the insertion point is somewhere in the first row. Then follow the preceding steps.

Converting a table to text

1. Select the row (or rows) or the entire table.

2. Choose Convert Table to Text from the Table menu to open the Convert Table to Text dialog box.

3. Choose how to separate the text. For columns of numbers, you probably should select tabs; for text, you probably should select paragraphs.

You can convert your table to text. You can use commas, tabs, or paragraph marks to separate the contents of each cell when they are converted to text. You can convert individual rows as well as the entire table.

The Convert Table to Text option is not available unless you first select either a row or the entire table.

Showing the gridlines

1. Choose Gridlines from the Table menu.

2. To make the gridlines show, be sure that a check mark appears next to Gridlines. Clear the check mark by selecting Gridlines to make the gridlines invisible.

The gridlines are just guidelines to assist you when you work in a table. You can elect to have them visible. If you format the gridlines to print, however, they always are visible on-screen.

Whether or not the gridlines are visible, they are still there. In other words, you can select rows and columns and cells regardless of whether the gridlines are visible.

Formatting the gridlines to print

1. Select the part of the table you want to format. If you want the gridlines to print for the entire table, select the entire table.
2. Choose Border from the Format menu.
3. Choose either Box or Grid in the Preset box at the bottom of the dialog box.
4. Choose the type of gridlines you want in the Line box.
5. Click on OK.

Many variations are possible here. If you select the entire table, you format all the gridlines to print. If you select just certain rows or columns, only the gridlines you select are formatted to be printed. You can also select all or part of the table to shade the contents of the selection. This is another feature you should play with until you get the feel of it.

You can achieve some nice effects here with a little imagination. For example, you can select every other column (which requires a separate operation for each selection) and format the left and right gridlines to print so that you then have vertical lines between your columns. Let your imagination run wild. (Well, at least let it off the leash for a while.)

Working in Tables

When you work with text or numbers in a table, you use normal formatting procedures. To center the contents of a cell, for example, you can click the Center button on the toolbar or choose Paragraph from the Format menu and then choose Centered in the Alignment box. The following table lists table keystrokes; the second table lists mouse actions you may find useful when you are working with a table.

Keystroke	Table Action
Enter	Inserts paragraphs in a cell
Tab	Moves to the next cell in a row
Shift+Tab	Moves to the preceding cell in a row
Alt+Home	Moves to the first cell in a row
Alt+End	Moves to the last cell in a row
Alt+Page Up	Moves to the top cell in a column
Alt+Page Down	Moves to the last cell in a column
Up- or down-arrow key	Moves to the next row up or down
Ctrl+Tab	Inserts a tab in a cell
Alt+5 (on the numeric keypad on the right side of the keyboard; the Num Lock light must be off)	Selects the entire table

Table Action	Mouse Action
Select a cell	Move the mouse pointer carefully to the left part of the cell until the pointer becomes an arrow that points toward the upper right, and then click once.
Select a row	A. Move the mouse pointer to the left of the row outside the table until the pointer becomes an arrow that points to the upper right and click once.
	B. Move the mouse pointer carefully to the left part of any cell in the row until the pointer becomes an arrow that points to the upper right, and then double-click.
Select a column	Move the mouse pointer anywhere in the column you want and click the right mouse button once.
Select entire table	Point at the first column, press the right button, and drag across all the columns in the table.

Tables and Tabs

Each cell of a table is similar to a paragraph. You can format a cell in exactly the same manner as you format a paragraph. If you are in a table, in fact, and you switch the ruler to indent scale (see Part II), you see that each cell has its own set of indent markers.

You may recall that there are two elements in general when you are working with tabs: the tab stop you insert on the ruler and the Tab key you press when you want to insert a tab in your text.

The most interesting fact about tables and tabs in Word for Windows is that, if you use decimal tabs in your table, you don't have to use the Tab key. In other words, decimal tabs work immediately. This capability makes number alignment in columns quite simple.

You should keep two important points in mind here:

- You must insert the decimal tab stop correctly over the selected column. If you want to insert decimal tab stops for multiple columns, you can select the columns and then enter the tab in the ruler *just once* over the leftmost selected column. The other columns you selected also have that tab stop in the correct place.

- If you find that the numbers in your table are not aligning correctly and you cannot get them aligned, you more than likely have decimal tab stops placed incorrectly in the table. An incorrectly placed decimal tab stop causes this effect. The easiest remedy is to choose Tabs from the Format menu and click the Clear All button in the Tabs dialog box. This step clears all the tab stops from the table so that you can begin again.

Other types of tab stops still require you to enter a tab in the cell in order for them to be effective.

For more information on using tables, See chapter 12.

Part VI
All About Merges in Word for Windows

The mail-merge feature is another strength of Word for Windows. It makes what used to be a very difficult task into one that is relatively easy (well, at least not as difficult).

You use a mail-merge tool when you want to send the same document to a number of different addresses. It would be extremely tedious, for example, to create 200 separate letters when the only difference in each letter is the address block.

Despite all the advances in the computer world, most printers still cannot handle envelopes well. Even the Word for Windows envelope feature is designed for single envelopes. Mailing labels, therefore, are still very much with us.

The process of creating mailing labels in Word for Windows is similar to performing a merge. There are some differences, but the idea is the same. You have two documents — the label document and the data file. You enter codes in the label document that tell Word for Windows the location of the data file and what information you want from it.

The Word for Windows approach to creating labels should save you a great deal of time and trouble. All you have to know is the Avery label product number of the type of labels you want to use, because that's what Word for Windows uses to construct the label layout.

Mail Merges and Labels

All merges work in a similar manner regardless of the software you use to create them. Two files are involved: the data file (known also as the database, the variable file, and the secondary file) and the main document (known also as the constant file, the letter document, and the primary file). Whatever name you call it, the principle remains the same.

The data file is really a *database,* which is a collection of records stored in a table. By using a database, you can be sure that each record has the same *structure,* regardless of whether each field contains data. The record structure is composed of fields. Each cell in the record is a *field.* The following figure shows an example of a basic data file. (Notice that the Title field is blank in the first record.)

Name Field	*Title Field*	*Company Field*	*Address Field*	*Record*
Name	Title	Company	Address	Header Record
John Doe		XYZ Corporation	123 Main Street Chicago, IL 12345	Record 1
Mary H. Lamb	Big Boss	Peep & Lamb	1405 Sunshine Blvd. Miami, FL 23456	Record 2

If you want to use a data file in a merge, the file cannot contain anything except records. The first record, called the *header record,* must be a description of the columns beneath it. If anything else is at the beginning of the data file, you receive an error message when you try to merge. You can use as many as 20 characters, including letters, numbers, and underscores for each field name. You cannot use spaces, and the first character must be a letter.

Your data file probably will include more information, of course, such as salutations, phone numbers, and other information.

For some unfortunate reason, Microsoft decided to add to Word for Windows an element called a header file. (Large mail-order companies that handle mass mailings use header files, but no one else does.) A *header file* is nothing more than a file that consists of one record — the header record. So unless you have the bad luck to actually use header files, you can ignore references to them.

The way a header file works is that, when you create the main document (the letter, for example), you insert codes in the letter that tell Word for Windows where to find the data file and in which part of each record to put each letter.

Creating a Merge

1. If you already have a letter you want to use as a main document, open it. It should be the active document.

   To create a main document, begin with a new, blank document.

 See the section "Preparing the Main Document" in Chapter 18 of *Word for Windows For Dummies*.

2. Choose Print Merge from the File menu to open the Print Merge Setup dialog box. The only buttons available to you are Attach Data File, Attach Header File, and Cancel. (As mentioned, all references to a header file are ignored).

3. Click the Attach Data File button to open the Attach Data File dialog box. Look familiar? It should. This dialog box is almost an exact replica of the File Open dialog box. The only difference is the Create Data File button in the lower-right corner.

   If you already have a data file and want to open it, you can use this dialog box. It works in exactly the same manner as the usual File Open dialog box.

4. To create a new data file, click the Create Data File button to open the Create Data File dialog box.

 See the section "Preparing the Data File" in Chapter 18 of *Word for Windows For Dummies*.

5. Use this dialog box to begin creating your table structure. Type a name in the Field Name box and then press Enter. This step adds that name to the list in the Fields in Header Record box. In this way, you construct the header record.

 It's a good idea to plan the structure of your data file. If you think that at some time in the future you may have to sort on some part of the database (names, ZIP codes, and states, for example), you have to create a separate field for that item. You may want to add a field for honorifics (Mr., Ms., Dr., and Professor, for example). It is also useful to add a field that contains whatever comes after Dear in the address block (Dear Mr. Smith or Dear John). Name these fields anything you want.

6. Repeat step 5 for each field you want in your data file.

7. When you have completed the process of adding field names, click on OK. This step opens the Save As dialog box.

Microsoft Word - TESTDATA.DOC

| File | Edit | View | Insert | Format | Tools | Table | Window | Help |

Sal	Fname	Lname	Title	Company	Address	City	State	Zip	Phone

8. Give the data file a name, select a drive and directory, and then click on OK. (Word for Windows has to know the name and location of your data file before it can attach it to your main document.) This step opens the data file, which displays a new toolbar and a table that consists of the header record and one blank record (see the following figure).

9. Begin entering your data. If you feel comfortable with tables, you can use the Word for Windows table features to build and maintain your data file. If you don't feel comfortable with tables, you can use the lettered buttons on the toolbar. The table that follows these steps explains each of the lettered buttons on the data file toolbar.

10. When you have finished entering your data, save it by choosing Save from the File menu (or by clicking on the third button from the left on the toolbar).

11. Now that your data file is built, return to the main document by clicking once on the M button. (M means Main — clever, isn't it?) Or you can select the main document from the Window menu. The main document now has a new toolbar just above the ruler (see the following figure).

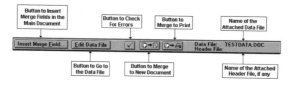

Button to Insert
Merge Fields in the
Main Document

Button to Check
For Errors

Button to
Merge to Print

Name of the
Attached Data File

Insert Merge Field... | Edit Data File | ✓ | ▯→▯ | ▯→🖨 | Data File: TESTDATA.DOC
                                                           Header File:

Button to Go to
the Data File

Button to Merge
to New Document

Name of the Attached
Header File, if any

12. Create the letter just as you would create any document. Every time you want to insert a field from the data file, click once on the Insert Merge Field button on the merge toolbar to open the Insert Merge Field dialog box.

13. Select the fields you want to include in the main document's address block. (Don't worry about the Word Fields box. The codes in this box are used only in special situations.) To begin the address block, for example, select the name field (or first name, if that's how you constructed your data file) and click on OK. Then add a return (or a space, depending on the structure of your data file), click on Insert Merge Field again, and select the next field, and so on. In this manner, you can construct your address block.

14. When you have finished, save your main document.

You can add fields anywhere in the main document, not just in the address block, if that's appropriate. You can use some fields and not others, if that's appropriate. You can also use a field more than once, if that's appropriate.

Letter	Meaning
A	Adds a new record to the data file. Word for Windows generates a series of dialog boxes you can use to enter information for each field in the record.
D	Deletes a record. You can delete the current record (where the insertion point currently is located) or enter a record number.
E	Edits a record. You can edit the current record (where the insertion point currently is) or enter a record number.
G	(Go To) Asks you for a record number and takes you to that record.
F	(Field) Displays a dialog box in which you can enter a new field name. Word for Windows adds that field as a new column to the end of the data file.
S	Sorts the records. Word for Windows displays a dialog box in which you can choose your sort criteria (Last Name, Company, State, and so on)
N	Numbers the records. If you click this button, Word for Windows inserts a column in front of the first column and then numbers all the records in the data file.
C	Cleans the data file. You can select from various criteria to have Word for Windows search for and delete certain types of errors.
L	Links the data file to other applications.
M	(Main document) Brings you to the main document.

Creating Mailing Labels

1. Choose New from the File menu to open the File New dialog box.

2. Choose MAILLABL in the Use Template box. *Do not* choose Template in the New box. (You're not creating a new template — you're creating a new file based on the MAILLABL template.)

3. Click on OK. At this point, Word for Windows opens a new document based on the MAILLABL template. A number of prompts follow.

4. When you are prompted, choose the type of printer (laser or dot-matrix).

5. Select the Avery product number for the type of label you want to use. As soon as you make this selection, Word for Windows constructs a table that matches the Avery label size and then asks you whether you want to print a single label or multiple labels.

6. Select whether you want to print just one label or multiple labels. If you select a single label, you add the information manually. If you select multiple labels, Word for Windows asks you whether your data is in both a header file and a data file. Unless you use header files, click on No.

7. Word for Windows opens the Attach Data File dialog box. If you have an existing data file, use this dialog box to open it. Otherwise, you can create one now. If you want to create a data file, follow steps 4 through 8 under the section "Creating a Merge," at the beginning of this part.

8. When you have named the file and clicked on OK to close the Save As dialog box, Word for Windows displays the Layout Mailing Labels dialog box.

9. Choose the first field name you want in each of your labels, and then choose a Special Character (a space, a new line, or a new paragraph, for example). Click on Add to Label.

10. Repeat step 9 for each field you want to add to your label. When you have added all the fields, click the Done button.

11. Word for Windows automatically adds the fields to each label in the table it constructed earlier (see step 5).

12. When Word for Windows finishes, it displays a reminder that you can begin the merge.

Even though you create only a single page of label codes, Word for Windows creates as many labels as you have records in your database.

Testing the Merge

The best way to test the merge is to merge to a new document. This process creates a merged file on the screen, as opposed to printing the merge. That way, you have a chance to inspect the merge results before you waste your time (and paper) printing it. You can either save or discard the merged result as you would do with any file.

1. Be sure that the main document (the letter or the label document) is the active document.

2. Click the checkmark button on the merge toolbar to be sure that there are no errors.

3. Choose Print Merge from the File menu to open the Print Merge Setup dialog box. Notice that all the buttons are now available, as shown in the following figure.

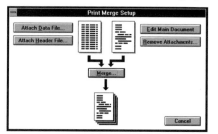

4. Click the Merge button in the center of the dialog box to open the Print Merge dialog box.

5. Select Merge to New Document in the Merge Results box. This step sends the result of the merge to the screen rather than to the printer.

6. In the Print Records box, enter records from 1 to 10, or any number you want. The idea is to run some records through the merge and have them appear on-screen so that you can inspect the result.

Notice, at the bottom of the dialog box, an area entitled Treatment of Blank Lines Caused by Empty Fields. Notice also that Skip Completely is selected. This means that Word for Windows does not print a blank line if, for example, a record has no entry in the Title field.

Running the Merge

After you have a main document (or a label document) and a data file and you have attached the data file to the main document, you can run the merge.

1. Be sure that the main document (the letter or the label document) is the active document.

2. Click the checkmark button on the merge toolbar to be sure that there are no errors.

3. Click the Merge to Print button (the last button) on the merge toolbar to send the merge to print.

 See "Merge Mania" in Chapter 18 of *Word for Windows For Dummies*.

Selecting Records for the Merge

You can also select certain records from your data file if you don't want to merge the entire file.

1. Be sure that the main document is active.

2. Choose Print Merge from the File menu to open the Print Merge dialog box. Notice that all the buttons are now available.

3. Click the Merge button in the center of the dialog box to open the Print Merge dialog box.

4. Click the Record Selection button to open the Record Selection dialog box.

5. Choose a field in the Field Name box, select a logical operand in the Is box, and then enter a value in the Compared To box. You can use this approach to select whatever records you need for the merge.

Removing Attachments

1. Be sure that the main document (or the label document) is active.

2. Choose Print Merge from the File menu to open the Print Merge dialog box. Notice that all the buttons are now available.

3. Click the Remove Attachments button. You receive a warning message that you are about to unattach the main document. Click on OK.

Merging attaches the data file to the main document. You can leave the attachment indefinitely so that, when you open the main document, Word for Windows prompts you to open the data file at the same time. Or you may have to unattach the main document, perhaps to attach it to a different data file.

If you closed your main document and data file without unattaching them, the next time you open the data document, Word for Windows prompts you to open the data file. Another option at this point is to remove the attachment, so it's no big deal if you forget after you do the original merge.

Part VII
Graphics and Pictures in Word for Windows

Maybe you remember when the only way to get a graphic into your document was to send that document to a print shop or a graphics artist. The good news is that now anyone can add graphics to a Word for Windows document. The bad news is that you have to learn more terms and concepts. (C'mon — it's not *that* bad. You can be the first one on your block to figure out how to do this stuff.)

Word for Windows comes with a bunch of small programs, called *applets,* that you can use to create and embed graphics in your document. The applets include Microsoft Draw (a cleverly named drawing program); Microsoft Graph (a cleverly named program you can use to build graphs based on numbers); Microsoft Equation Editor (a cleverly named program you can use to create complex equations); and Microsoft WordArt (a cleverly named program that has unusual formatting options for text).

OLE, an acronym for Object Linking and Embedding, has to do with the exchange of information between different applications. You can find out more about OLE in this part.

Using Graphics

Several methods are available for adding graphics to a Word for Windows document. You can use the graphics that come with Word for Windows (stored in the CLIPART directory); use the graphics that come with other software packages; create your own graphics by using the Word for Windows tools (known as *applets*); and create your own graphics by using other software packages. Any (or all) of these approaches works well in Word for Windows.

There are even ways to *link,* or connect, the graphics object in Word for Windows to the original graphic. By doing this, you can make changes in the original, and Word for Windows updates those changes in your document.

Then there's another procedure, called *embedding,* in which you can store an object in a Word for Windows document and update it by double-clicking on it. Double-clicking on an embedded object opens the application that created the object and lets you modify the object and update it in Word for Windows.

All this is pretty good stuff, so let's see how it works. This section shows you how to use graphics in Word for Windows.

Inserting (importing) graphics

You use the insertion procedure to insert a picture in your Word for Windows document. Chapter 19 in *Word for Windows For Dummies* covers this topic in more detail.

1. Choose Picture from the Insert menu to open the Insert Picture dialog box.
2. Select the drive and directory in which the file you want is stored. If you don't have a particular file in mind, switch to the CLIPART directory under WINWORD. This directory contains clip-art files that come with Word for Windows.
3. Select a file by clicking on it once.
4. To see a preview of the file before you insert it, click the Preview button.
5. To link the picture, click on the Link to File box. This step links the graphics file to the graphic you insert in the Word for Windows document. You can use the Links option from the Edit menu to update the link later, if necessary.
6. Click to insert the graphic.

The following table lists the types of graphics files that Word for Windows accepts.

File Extension	File Type
.bmp	Windows Bitmap
.cgm	Computer Graphics Metafile
.drw	Micrografx Designer/Draw
.dxf	AutoCAD Format 2-D
.eps	Encapsulated PostScript
.hgl	HP Graphic Language (HPGL)
.ima	Zenographics Mirage
.pcx	PC Paintbrush
.pic	Video Show Import
.plc	Lotus 1-2-3 graphics
.plt	AutoCAD Import
.plt	AutoCAD Plot File
.tif	Tagged Image Format
.tif	TIFF
.wmf	Windows Metafile
.wpg	DrawPerfect

Cropping and scaling pictures

1. Select the picture. Be careful not to double-click on the picture, because that causes Draw to open.
2. Choose Picture from the Format menu to open the Picture dialog box.
3. To crop the picture, either enter values or use the arrow buttons to the right of the boxes.
4. To scale the picture, either enter values or use the arrow buttons to the right of the boxes.
5. To return a cropped or scaled picture to its original size, click the Reset button.

You cannot, of course, crop or scale a picture if you don't have one in your document. Even if you do have one, you must select it before you can scale or crop it.

When you *crop* a picture, you trim it; when you *scale* a picture, you proportionally resize it. If you crop a picture in Word for Windows and then decide that you shouldn't have cropped it, the entire picture is still available to you. You can also use cropping to increase the white space around the picture (think of it as cropping in reverse). Finally, if you crop a picture, Word for Windows may change its position (yes, you can change it back by using the paragraph formatting tools).

Using the mouse to crop and scale is more efficient. When you first select the picture, it becomes outlined by light gray lines that have little squares (called *handles*) on them. If you place the mouse pointer on a handle and click and drag, you scale the picture. To scale the height and width proportionally, be sure to click on a corner handle (most people use the bottom right handle). To crop, just hold down Shift while you use the mouse.

Positioning (framing) graphics

1. Select the item you want to position.
2. Click once on the Frame button on the toolbar (the 14th button from the left).
3. In normal view, Word for Windows displays a message asking whether you want to switch to page layout view. Click the Yes button. The framed object then is displayed in page layout view.
4. Move the mouse pointer slowly into the framed object. Notice that it changes to a four-headed arrow. It takes this shape to indicate when you can click and drag on a framed object.
5. Click and drag on the framed object to move it to the position you want on the page. If you drop the object into a paragraph, the text automatically wraps around it.

You can precisely position paragraphs, tables, and graphics in your document by selecting the item and inserting it in a frame. Then you position the frame where you want. You cannot see framed objects in their correct position in normal view, but you can see them in page layout view.

Framing is the process of positioning items on a particular page, so you should be sure first that the item you want to frame is on the correct page.

If you view a framed object in normal view, the object doesn't appear in the correct position on the page. A black square dot is displayed to its left. That's how you can tell a framed object when you are in normal view.

The Format Frame dialog box

1. Select the framed object.
2. Choose Frame from the Format menu. If it isn't available, either you didn't select a framed object or the object you thought was framed is not framed. This step opens the Format Frame dialog box.
3. In the Text Wrapping box, choose whether you want the text to flow around the framed object.
4. The Size box sets the width and height of the frame. It's probably best to leave this setting on Auto.
5. From the Horizontal and Vertical boxes, you set the horizontal and vertical position of the frame, and select what the frame should be relative to (margin, edge of page, or from within a column).
6. To remove the frame, click the Remove Frame button.
7. When you finish, click on OK.

After you have inserted a frame around an object, you can modify a number of elements about the frame, such as the way you want text outside the frame to wrap around the object, the exact position of the framed object on the page, and whether to remove the frame. You can do all this from the Format Frame dialog box, which you may find a bit tedious to use. Chapter 19 covers this feature in detail.

Those Amazing Applets

Because some of the Word for Windows applets are almost full-fledged programs in themselves, you probably will have to practice before you become proficient in using them. They all share one major characteristic: You cannot save in a separate file anything you create in them. You just use them to create objects embedded in your Word for Windows document. As a matter of fact, you cannot even open them unless you are in Word for Windows (or some other application, such as Excel, that can use them — which is probably why they are called applets rather than applications).

Because a discussion of the use of the applets exceeds the scope of this book, none of them is covered in detail here. (See Chapter 20 for the details on Applets.) If you want to try using them, open one and play with it. Try WordArt — it is probably the easiest to learn and the most fun to use. When you have an applet open, you can get extensive help in using it by just pressing F1.

1. Choose Object from the Insert menu to open the Insert Object dialog box.
2. Select the applet you want and click on OK.

Microsoft Draw

You use Microsoft Draw, a basic drawing program, to create and edit graphics. You can open clip-art files and modify them by using Draw. The following figure shows the Draw window.

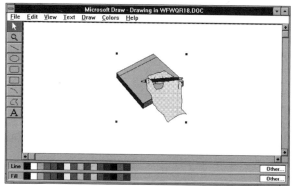

Microsoft Equation Editor

Use the Microsoft Equation Editor applet to create and edit equations of almost any complexity. The following figure shows an example of an equation created in the Equation Editor.

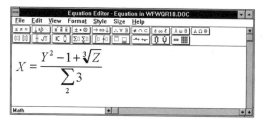

Microsoft Graph

With the Microsoft Graph basic charting program, you can create charts and graphs based on numbers you enter in its spreadsheet layout. You can also first select a numeric table you have in your document and then Graph charts that table instead. The following figure shows an example of a graph in the Graph window.

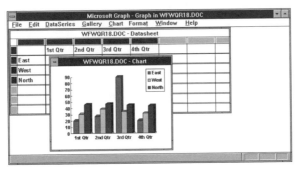

Microsoft WordArt

Use the WordArt feature to create, modify, and enhance text. Word for Windows treats the text you create in WordArt not as text but rather as a graphic. The following figure shows an example of an object created in WordArt. The border was created by using Forma_t _Border.

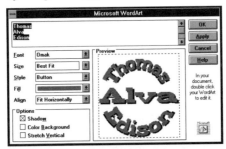

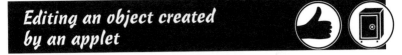

Editing an object created by an applet

1. Double-click on the object to open the applet that created it.
2. Make your changes.
3. Choose _Update from the _File menu. (WordArt does not have a file menu, so just click on either the _Apply button or the OK button. _Apply applies the changes without closing WordArt.)
4. Close the applet.

Linking and Embedding

You may have noticed computer nerds and geeks recently using the term *OLE* (pronounced O-LAY). No, they aren't practicing bullfighting — what respectable nerd or geek would do such a thing?) Instead, they are engaging in the time-honored practice of using buzzwords. Some people think that a buzzword is a word with a specific meaning in a specific industry. It's really a word that many people use to engage in another time-honored practice: one-upsmanship. Now you have at least some idea of what this particular buzzword means.

OLE, or Object Linking and Embedding, has to do with the exchange of information between different applications. Although they are similar, linking is a little different from embedding. You cannot link or embed by using applications that don't have linking or embedding capabilities. This statement eliminates all non-Windows applications. Too bad, WordPerfect 5.1 and 6.0 users.

You can see the linking and embedding field codes by choosing Field Codes from the View menu. The objects disappear and the codes appear. Whether you display the codes or the object, only the object is printed.

When you link, you use one application (such as Excel) to create an object (such as a table or chart) that you use in another application (such as Word for Windows). If you just copied the object from one application to another and didn't establish a link, each piece of that object (the piece in Excel and the piece in Word for Windows) would be static. In other words, if you open Excel and make a change to that object, you have to do the same thing in Word for Windows if you want to be sure that the two objects match. Tedious, at best.

When you link the information, however, any change you make in Excel to the object also occurs in Word for Windows. Not bad, eh? So, linking means that you have at least two applications: the one that created the object and the one that gets the object. (You can create links between more than two applications.)

You can also update the information in the receiving (or destination) application independently; if you do, however, the next time you update the links, that update overwrites any changes you made independently. Got that? You can permanently break the link so that updating a link doesn't change any independent changes you make.

Embedding is different in a couple of ways. First, although you still create the object in a different application, rather than link it, you choose to embed it. This means that the object is not saved in the application that created it. Instead, the object just exists now in Word for Windows. So, how do you update it? When you embed an object, all the information used to create the object is stored with it.

To update the embedded object, all you have to do is double-click on it. When you double-click, the application that created it opens automatically and displays that object. You can use the application's tools and features, therefore, to make changes to the object. When you close the application, the object in Word for Windows is updated with the changes you made.

Creating a link

To create a link, of course, you first have to create something in another application, such as Excel.

1. Begin by making active the application you want to use to create the object.
2. Select the object.
3. Choose Copy from the Edit menu. This step puts the object on the Clipboard. (All Windows applications that support linking have an Edit Copy option.)
4. Switch to Word for Windows.
5. Choose Paste Special from the Edit menu. This step displays the Paste Special dialog box. (Choosing Paste simply inserts a static copy of the object in your Word for Windows document. You don't want that, do you?) The following table explains each of the options in the Paste Special dialog box.
6. Choose the Data Type option and then click the Paste Link button. That's what establishes the link.

Option	Explanation
Object (this example shows Excel worksheet)	Embeds the object (the Paste Link button is not available because you cannot paste and embed at the same time)
Formatted Text (RTF)	Places the Excel table in Word for Windows as a formatted Word for Windows table
Unformatted Text	Places the Excel table in Word for Windows as a tabbed table
Picture	A picture representation of the object
Bitmap	A picture representation used by Paintbrush

Embedding an object

1. Choose Object from the Edit menu to open the Insert Object dialog box.
2. Choose the application in which you want to create the object and then click on OK.
3. When you have finished creating the object, in most applications you can choose Update from the File menu. Or, just close the application. A prompt appears and asks whether you want to update Word for Windows. Say Yes or OK. The embedded object appears at the position of the insertion point.

You can see from the preceding table that one method of embedding is to create the object in the other application, copy it to the Clipboard, open the Paste Special dialog box in Word for Windows, and then select Object. This method, however, is not the most common one — that one was described in these steps.

Editing a link

1. Choose Links from the Edit menu to open the Edit Links dialog box, which displays all the linked objects in your document. (If Edit Links isn't available, your document has no links.)
2. Use this dialog box to modify the characteristics of a particular link. Press F1 to get help in using the various options. The following figure shows the Links dialog box.

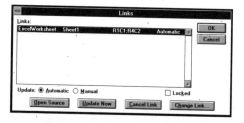

Updating a linked object

1. Open the application that created the linked object.
2. Open the file that contains the linked object.
3. Make the changes. They automatically occur in the linked object in Word for Windows. (If you want to change that, see the preceding section, "Editing a link.")

Updating an embedded object

1. Double-click on the embedded object to open the application in which it was created.
2. Make the changes to the object.
3. Choose Update from the File menu, or just simply close the application.

Part VII:
Printing

What can we say about printing? If your printer is installed properly (that's done through Windows, not through Word for Windows), you should have no trouble printing your documents.

Printing Documents

1. Choose Print from the File menu to open the Print dialog box.
2. In the Print box, select what you want to print (the document, summary info, annotations, styles, glossaries, and key assignments).
3. Choose the number of copies you want.
4. Select a range if you want to print part of your document.
5. Click on OK. The printing process begins.

What can you say about printing? If your printer is installed properly (you do that from Windows, not from Word for Windows), you should have no trouble printing.

To print multiple documents, you can use File Find File (see Part III).

Selecting a Different Printer

1. Choose Print from the File menu to open the Print dialog box.
2. Click the Setup button to open the Print Setup dialog box.
3. Choose the printer you want to use and click on OK to return to the Print dialog box, from which you can print your document.

You cannot select a different printer unless another printer was installed through Windows. If you have more than one printer installed, you can choose which printer you want to use to print your document.

Setting Print Options

1. Choose Print from the File menu to open the Print dialog box.
2. Click the Options button to open the Print Options dialog box.
3. Choose the options you want and click on OK to return to the Print dialog box, from which you can print your document.

You can set various print options, such as printing summary info, field codes, annotations, and hidden text, to print with your document. You can also set Widow/Orphan Control (see "Setting Orphan and Window Control"). The following figure shows the Print Options dialog box.

```
                              Options
 Category:               Adjust print settings
 ┌─────────┐ ┌─Printing Options─┐ ┌─Include with Document─┐  ┌──────────┐
 │   [🖨]   │ │ ☐ Draft Output   │ │ ☐ Summary Info        │  │    OK    │
 │  Print  │ │ ☐ Reverse Print Order │ ☐ Field Codes      │  ├──────────┤
 └─────────┘ │ ☐ Update Fields  │ │ ☐ Annotations         │  │  Cancel  │
             └──────────────────┘ │ ☐ Hidden Text         │  └──────────┘
                                  └───────────────────────┘
             ┌─Envelope Options────────────────────────────┐
             │ ☐ Printer's Envelope Feeder has been Installed │
             └─────────────────────────────────────────────┘
             ┌─Options for Current Document Only───────────┐
             │ ☒ Widow/Orphan Control                      │
             │ ☐ Use TrueType Fonts as Defaults            │
             └─────────────────────────────────────────────┘
```

Printing Selections

1. Select the portion of the document you want to print.
2. Choose Print from the File menu to open the Print dialog box. The Current Page option will have changes to Selection.
3. Choose the Selection option.
4. Click on OK.

You can print just a portion of the document you first select. If you print a selection, however, headers and footers are not printed and page breaks are not printed correctly.

Setting Orphan and Widow Control

Widow and orphan control refers to the process of taking widows and orphans into the woods and executing them. (No, not really.) In word processing and in desktop publishing, widows and orphans refer to the way that paragraphs with a page break in them are printed. It's contrary to desktop publishing convention to have only one line from a multiline paragraph at the bottom of a page or at the top of a page. You should have at least two lines there.

One of the options you can turn on in the Print Options dialog box is Widow/Orphan Control. If this option is on, Word for Windows adjusts all page breaks so that at least two lines of a multiline paragraph appear at the bottom or top of a page.

Printing Envelopes

1. If your printer has an envelope feeder installed, choose that option in the Print Options dialog box. Otherwise, use the manual feeder for your printer.

2. If you have a document open that has an address, select the address. Word for Windows automatically takes this address as the envelope's address block. Otherwise, continue to step 3.

3. Choose Create Envelope from the Tools menu to open the Create Envelope dialog box. Or, click the envelope button on the toolbar (the sixth button from the right).

4. Type the address in the Addressed To box. (If you have selected an address in step 2, that address already appears in the box.)

5. Enter the return address in the Return Address box.

 Word for Windows automatically adds a return address if you complete the User Info options. To do this, choose Options from the Tools menu to open the Options dialog box. Then choose User Info from the list of categories on the left (you may have to scroll to see this category). Enter the user information.

6. If you don't want a return address to be printed (if you use preprinted envelopes, for example), click in the Omit Return Address box.

7. Choose the envelope size you want from the Envelope Size box.

 8. Click the Print Envelope button.

For more information on printing, see *Word for Windows For Dummies*, Chapters 8 and 24.

Part IX:
Very Advanced Stuff —
Fields and Macros

This part describes two of Word for Windows most advanced features: fields and macros. If you want to become a power user in Word for Windows someday, you eventually must come to terms with these topics. For everyday use of Word for Windows, however, there is no need to worry about these things. You can live a full life without ever reading up on fields or creating a macro.

Fields

Fields are codes you can use to enter and display information or settings, such as the time and date and the page number. You can enter these items by typing them, of course, but then you have to worry about date changes or page changes. If you use fields, Word for Windows takes care of it all for you. For more information, see Chapter 18, "Mail Merge for the Mental," in *Word for Windows For Dummies.*

Field codes are also used in merges. If you choose Field Codes from the View menu when you have a merge document active, you can see the underlying codes that Word for Windows uses.

A field code generally has two parts: the code and the result of the code. Another way of saying this is that you can see either the date or the code that causes the date to appear. Regardless of whether you have View Field Codes on, only the result of the field code is printed (unless you select Field Codes from the File Print Options dialog box).

Most processes that use basic fields in Word for Windows are very easy. When you insert the date or time from the Insert menu, for example, you insert a field code that causes the date and time to appear.

Field codes appear in field braces, which are not the same as the braces you can type from the keyboard (although they look the same). Field code braces are special braces you can generate by pressing Ctrl+F9.

Before you use this option, you should be knowledgeable about fields and the different field types in Word for Windows.

Inserting fields from the menu

1. Choose Field from the Insert menu to open the Field dialog box (See the following figure).
2. Select the field you want to insert from the Insert Field Type box. Notice that a one-line description appears below the Field Code box at the bottom of the dialog box. If the field you choose has to be formatted, the available formats appear in the Instructions box.
3. Click OK. The field you selected is inserted at the insertion point.

TIP

You can get information about each field in the Insert Field dialog box by opening the dialog box, choosing the field you are interested in, and pressing F1.

Field		
Insert Field Type:	Instructions:	OK
= expression	#,##0	Cancel
Ask	#,##0.00	Add
Author	$#,##0.00;($#,##0.00)	
Auto No.	0	
Auto No. legal	0%	
Auto No. outline	0.00	
Comments	0.00%	

Field Code: = expression

=

Select format; then type numeric expression.

Inserting fields from the keyboard

If you use a particular field frequently, you will be pleased to know that you don't always have to use the menus to insert the field.

1. Press Ctrl+F9. Field braces appear in the document, and the insertion point is inside the braces.
2. Type the name of the field.
3. Move the insertion point out of the braces.

To insert the page number field, for example, press Ctrl+F9 and type **PAGE**. Then move the insertion point out of the braces and continue with whatever you were doing.

Viewing field codes

1. Choose Field Codes from the View menu. This step puts a checkmark next to the Field Codes option.
2. Scroll through your document to look for the field codes.
3. To turn off Field Codes, repeat step 1. The checkmark disappears and you do not see the codes — only the field results.

You can have field codes in a document and not even know it. Or, you may need to locate a particular field in order to delete or modify it.

Macros

Funny word, "macro." It used to mean the opposite of micro, but now it has a whole new meaning. The meaning varies, depending on the software you use. For more information on macros, see Chapter 29, "Ten Features You Don't Use but Paid for Anyway," in *Word for Windows For Dummies*.

In Word for Windows, macros can range from a recording of keystrokes to full-blown programs. Professional developers use Word for Windows' own programming language to create macros that do all sorts of nifty things. (You probably didn't know that Word for Windows has its own programming language. From the Help menu, choose Help Index and look at the last item in the Help Index window.) The use of the Word for Windows programming language is an advanced skill, and entire books have been written about it.

You can use the Word for Windows macro recorder, however, to record a series of keystrokes. The easy-to-use macro recorder translates your keystroke actions into the Word Programming Language for you, so you don't have to worry about creating a program. Although you cannot record mouse actions, you can use the mouse to select options while recording a macro.

When you have recorded the macro and given it a name, you can assign a keystroke combination to execute the macro and you can assign it to a menu or create a button for it on the toolbar.

You can use this feature to your advantage, especially for repetitive tasks. If you commonly have to insert a section break and change the margins in many of your documents, for example, you can record a macro to do it for you. Then, if you have assigned it a keystroke combination, when you next need to insert the section break and change the margins, you just use the keystroke. Voila! The task is completed.

If you are working in a document created with a template other than the Normal template, when you begin to record the macro, Word for Windows asks you where you want to store the macro — in the current template or in the Normal template. Storing the macro in the Normal template makes it available for use in any document based on the Normal template. Storing the macro in a custom template makes it available for use only in documents based on that template.

Creating a macro by using the macro recorder

1. Choose Record Macro from the Tools menu to open the Record Macro dialog box.
2. Type a name for your macro in the Record Macro Name box.
3. If you want to use a shortcut keystroke for your macro, assign one in the Shortcut Key box. Word for Windows tells you whether the keystroke you choose is currently unassigned.
4. Enter a brief description of the macro in the Description box.
5. Click on OK. Notice that the letters REC appear in the status bar, to indicate that you are in macro record mode.
6. Perform the actions you want to include in the macro.

7. When you have finished with your actions, choose Stop Recorder from the Tools menu. *Don't forget to turn off the recorder.*

Running a macro

1. Choose Macro from the Tools menu to open the Macro dialog box.

2. Notice the Show box on the right. If you have saved your macro previously in a template, choose Template Macros. If you have saved it to the Normal template, choose Global Macros. (If you choose Commands, you see the macros Word for Windows uses to perform its functions. *Do yourself a favor and leave these macros alone.*)

3. Select your macro when it appears in the box under Macro Name. When you select the macro, the buttons on the right become available. In addition to running the macro, you can edit, delete, and rename it.

4. Choose Run. The macro will run.

There are several ways to run a macro you have created. If you have assigned the macro to the toolbar, you can run it by clicking on the appropriate button. If you have assigned the macro to a menu, you can run it by choosing it from the menu. If you have assigned a keystroke combination to the macro, you can run the macro by using the keystroke combination. You can also run the macro from the Tools menu (explained in the preceding steps). *No matter which method you choose, you should save your document first in case the result is not what you expect.*

If you choose Edit, Word for Windows opens the macro editing window, which may cause some confusion because it looks so different. If this happens, just choose Close from the File menu.

Assigning and removing a keystroke shortcut to a macro

1. Choose Options from the Tools menu to open the Tools Options dialog box.

2. In the Tools Options dialog box, select Keyboard from the categories on the left. You may have to scroll to see this category. This step opens the Keyboard Options dialog box.

3. Choose either Global or Template in the Context box on the right, depending on how you created your macro.

4. Choose Macros in the Show box.

5. Select your macro from the list in the Macros box.

6. If any current keystrokes are assigned to the macro, they show up in the Current Keys For box.

7. Assign the keystroke in the Shortcut Key box. If you select a keystroke that is in use, the current use shows up next to Currently. It's best to choose a keystroke combination that isn't in use.

8. Click the Add button.

9. Repeat steps 3 through 8 for each macro to which you want to assign a shortcut keystroke.

10. Click Close.

11. You can remove any assignments later by opening the same dialog box and clicking the Reset All button.

Assigning and removing a macro to a menu

1. Choose Options from the Tools menu to open the Tools Options dialog box.

2. In the Tools Options dialog box, select Menus from the categories on the left. You may have to scroll to see Menus. This step opens the Menus Options dialog box.

3. Choose either Global or Template in the Context box on the right, depending on how you created your macro.

4. Choose Macros in the Show box.

5. Select the menu you want to put the macro on by clicking the down arrow to the right of the Menu box.

6. When you have selected the menu for your macro, select the line of dashes if you want your macro separated from the other menu items by this type of line. Otherwise, just select the macro in the Macros box. The macro title appears in the box under Menu Text, and the Add button becomes available.

7. Click the Add button and then click Close. Your macro appears on the menu you chose, at the bottom. If you have assigned a shortcut keystroke, it appears also.

8. You can remove any assignments later by opening the same dialog box and clicking the Reset All button.

Assigning and removing a macro to the toolbar

1. Choose Options from the Tools menu to open the Tools Options dialog box.

2. In the Tools Options dialog box, select Toolbar from the categories on the left. You may have to scroll to see this category. This step opens the Toolbar Options dialog box.

3. Choose either Global or Template in the Context box on the right, depending on how you created your macro.

4. Choose Macros in the Show box.

5. Choose the macro from the list in the Macros window.

6. Select from the Button list a button that you want to represent your macro on the toolbar. Scroll through the list to see all the available buttons.

7. Select the Tool to Change option from the toolbar by clicking the down arrow to the right of the Tool to Change box. This step opens a list of tools on the toolbar. Each tool on the list corresponds to a current tool on the toolbar. Because FileNewDefault is the first button on the toolbar, for example, if you select that tool, you replace the first button on the toolbar with your macro.

8. When you have selected the tool (including any space you're lucky enough to find), click the Change button. Your new tool appears immediately on the toolbar.

9. When you have completed all your assignments, click Close.

10. You can remove any assignments later by opening the same dialog box and clicking the Reset All button.

You cannot really add anything to the Word for Windows toolbar — instead, you replace something that is already on the toolbar. Fortunately, you can replace spaces, so you can, in effect, add your macro to the toolbar without removing any of the current buttons.

Part X
Taking the Shortcut Route

This part lists the shortcut keystroke combinations you can press to make performing tasks easier and quicker in your Word for Windows documents.

Shortcut Keystrokes

As the following table shows, you can press the Ctrl key first and then press the character in the first column to produce the effect shown in the second column. The table shows both paragraph and character formatting keys you can use in Word for Windows.

Keystroke (Ctrl+)	Action
Paragraph formatting	
E	Center
G	Unhang indent
J	Justify
L	Left align
M	Unnest
N	Nest
O	Open space before
Q	Return to style format
R	Right align
S	Style
T	Hanging indent
0	Close space before
1	Single spacing
2	Double spacing
5	1 1/2-inch line spacing
Character formatting	
A	All caps
B	Bold
D	Double underline
F	Font
H	Hidden
I	Italic
K	Small caps
P	Point size
U	Continuous underline

Keystroke (Ctrl+)	Action
W	Word underline
Spacebar	Reset character
=	Subscript
+	Superscript

The next table shows some other shortcut keystrokes you can use to perform tasks in Word for Windows.

Keystroke	*Action*
Ctrl+C	Copy
Ctrl+V	Paste
Ctrl+X	Cut
Esc	Cancel
Enter	Begin new paragraph
Shift+Enter	Begin new line
Ctrl+Enter	Begin new page
Ctrl+Shift+Enter	Begin new column or split table
Ctrl+Hyphen	Insert optional hyphen
Ctrl+Shift+Spacebar	Insert nonbreaking space
Tab	Move to next cell in table
Ctrl+Tab	Tab character in table
Ctrl+*	Show nonprinting characters

For a listing of frequently used shortcut keys, see Chapter 30, "Ten Shortcut Keys Worth Remembering," in *Word for Windows For Dummies*.

Index

Order Form

Order Center: (800) 762-2974 (8 a.m.-5 p.m. PST, weekdays)
For fastest service, photocopy this order form and fax to: (415) 358-1260

Qty	ISBN	Title	Price	Total

Shipping & Handling Charges

Subtotal	U.S.	Canada & International	International Air Mail
Up to $20.00	Add $3.00	Add $4.00	Add $10.00
$20.01-40.00	$4.00	$5.00	$20.00
$40.01-60.00	$5.00	$6.00	$25.00
$60.01-80.00	$6.00	$8.00	$35.00
Over $80.00	$7.00	$10.00	$50.00

In U.S. and Canada, shipping is UPS ground or equivalent.
For Rush shipping call (800) 762-2974.

Subtotal	_____
CA residents add applicable sales tax	_____
IN residents add 5% sales tax	_____
Canadian residents add 7% GST tax	_____
Shipping	_____
TOTAL	_____

Ship to:

Name _____

Company _____

Address _____

City/State/Zip _____

Daytime Phone _____

Payment: ❏ Check to IDG Books (US Funds Only) ❏ Visa ❏ MasterCard ❏ AMEX

Card # _____ Exp._____

Signature _____

Please send this order form to: IDG Books, 155 Bovet Road, Suite 310, San Mateo, CA 94402.
Allow up to 3 weeks for delivery. Thank you!

IDG BOOKS WORLDWIDE REGISTRATION CARD

RETURN THIS REGISTRATION CARD FOR FREE CATALOG

Title of this book: Word for Windows For Dummies Quick Reference

My overall rating of this book: ❏ Very good [1] ❏ Good [2] ❏ Satisfactory [3] ❏ Fair [4] ❏ Poor [5]

How I first heard about this book:
❏ Found in bookstore; name: [6]   ❏ Book review: [7]

❏ Advertisement: [8]   ❏ Catalog: [9]

❏ Word of mouth; heard about book from friend, co-worker, etc.: [10] ❏ Other: [11]

What I liked most about this book:

What I would change, add, delete, etc., in future editions of this book:

Other comments:

Number of computer books I purchase in a year: ❏ 1 [12] ❏ 2-5 [13] ❏ 6-10 [14] ❏ More than 10 [15]

I would characterize my computer skills as: ❏ Beginner [16] ❏ Intermediate [17] ❏ Advanced [18] ❏ Professional [19]

I use ❏ DOS [20] ❏ Windows [21] ❏ OS/2 [22] ❏ Unix [23] ❏ Macintosh [24] ❏ Other: [25]_____
(please specify)

I would be interested in new books on the following subjects:
(please check all that apply, and use the spaces provided to identify specific software)

❏ Word processing: [26]   ❏ Spreadsheets: [27]

❏ Data bases: [28]   ❏ Desktop publishing: [29]

❏ File Utilities: [30]   ❏ Money management: [31]

❏ Networking: [32]   ❏ Programming languages: [33]

❏ Other: [34]

I use a PC at (please check all that apply): ❏ home [35] ❏ work [36] ❏ school [37] ❏ other: [38] _____

The disks I prefer to use are ❏ 5.25 [39] ❏ 3.5 [40] ❏ other: [41]_____

I have a CD ROM: ❏ yes [42] ❏ no [43]

I plan to buy or upgrade computer hardware this year: ❏ yes [44] ❏ no [45]

I plan to buy or upgrade computer software this year: ❏ yes [46] ❏ no [47]

Name: _____ Business title: [48]

Type of Business: [49]

Address (❏ home [50] ❏ work [51]/Company name: _____

Street/Suite#

City [52]/State [53]/Zipcode [54]: _____ Country [55]

❏ **I liked this book!**
You may quote me by name in future IDG Books Worldwide promotional materials.

My daytime phone number is _____

IDG BOOKS

THE WORLD OF COMPUTER KNOWLEDGE

❏ YES!

Please keep me informed about IDG's World of Computer Knowledge. Send me the latest IDG Books catalog.